OP

1st US FD   7.50
              RY
              NA

D1257409

A PEACOCK ON THE LAWN

A PEACOCK
ON THE
LAWN

Anna Hadfield

LITTLE, BROWN AND COMPANY · BOSTON · TORONTO

COPYRIGHT © 1965, BY PHYLLIS ANNA HADFIELD

ALL RIGHTS RESERVED. NO PART OF THIS BOOK MAY BE REPRO-
DUCED IN ANY FORM WITHOUT PERMISSION IN WRITING FROM THE
PUBLISHER, EXCEPT BY A REVIEWER WHO MAY QUOTE BRIEF PAS-
SAGES IN A REVIEW TO BE PRINTED IN A MAGAZINE OR NEWSPAPER.

LIBRARY OF CONGRESS CATALOG CARD NO. 65-18132

FIRST AMERICAN EDITION

PRINTED IN THE UNITED STATES OF AMERICA

FOR JOHN

Author's note   Although this book is a straightforward record of fact I have found it easier to write about my friends and neighbours by giving them fictitious names. I hope they won't mind.

ILLUSTRATIONS

The photograph facing p. 48 is by F. L. Bantick; that facing p. 112 is by courtesy of *The East Anglian Magazine*; and those facing pages 17, 65, 81 and 128 are by John Hadfield. The others are by Miles Hadfield.

A PEACOCK ON THE LAWN

'WHAT this place needs,' said Miles, my brother-in-law, 'is a peacock on the lawn.'

It was a fine, late summer day in 1952. Big white clouds careered across the pale blue East Anglian sky, but never hid the sun for more than a few seconds. The air was crisp and sweet, with a faint tang of salt. But the sight of red berries in the hedgerows, a faint smoke haze from burning stubble, and the sound, endearing if rather didactic, of a robin's song, made me say to myself: 'It is later than you think.'

This was our first visit to the Manor since we had actually bought the old red brick Tudor House, and we were standing on a lawn that was neither spacious nor sweeping, but rather small and enclosed. However, being a gardening expert, Miles was already, I think, visualizing the removal of the rather scruffy Lonicera hedge, that grew too close to the house, and the extension of the lawn. John's imagination, I know, was doing far more than that. It was roaming around the garden, completely altering everything: chopping down trees, designing flights of steps, building walls and gazebos, and planting a dozen or so yew hedges. To say that John is fundamentally an optimist is perhaps an understatement.

I myself was still suffering from shock. Being a conservative person, I had not been entirely whole-hearted about moving at all, and I do not think I had really expected the owner of the Manor to accept our offer. Perhaps I had half hoped he wouldn't.

John and I had been unavailingly hunting for the 'perfect' house for some time. We had got to the point of saying, 'Well, if we don't get that house we will give up the hunt, settle down in our cottage, and perhaps build on to it.' We were in this resigned and perhaps slightly relieved frame of mind when we received the telephone message that told us we had bought the manor house. I was aghast at our temerity. Two stiff drinks did not entirely remove my apprehension.

We loved our Hertfordshire cottage, small though it was;

and the yew hedges there, which John had planted in 1940, in defiance of Hitler, had reached perfection. We had lived there for nearly thirteen years and, in spite of the war years with their burden of separations and anxieties, we had known much happiness and contentment in our village life, among so many good friends. But when John's health made it plain that he should not work all week in a town, it seemed foolish to continue living near to London, when we could buy a larger house in the 'real' country for far less money than we should get for our cottage when we sold it. At least, that was the theory!

We had chosen Suffolk as being real country and less fashionable, and we had friends in the county. Also, having been used to one, we were determined to have an old house, and there are more beautiful old houses in Suffolk to the square mile than in almost any other county. We did need a bigger house. We were cramped in the cottage, and now that John had to earn our living by his pen and his wits, he had to have a proper room to work in. But I think that, almost imperceptibly, our ideas had become a little grandiose. This wasn't big enough, or had a thatched roof; that had a nissen hut in the garden and was too close to other houses. Or perhaps the house under consideration had been too much or too badly altered from the original: we had become rather purist in our architectural ideas. At last an estate agent in Ipswich, desperately trying to please these choosy clients, said, 'What you want is this manor house I'm going to send you to.'

When we had driven the mile up the lane, the dusty road winding between tall hedges, and had left the ancient grey church behind, all we could see of the house, hidden as it was among huge elms, was its eight tall, octagonal chimneys, complete and unspoilt. 'This is it,' we said, gazing at one another in amazement and disbelief.

It was some time before I grasped the house in its entirety, so to speak, or noticed much else besides those eight beautiful

Tudor chimneys. They certainly sold the house to me. I couldn't, of course, foresee the many days when, having opened up and restored the big, open fireplaces with their Tudor arches, we should curse those same chimneys for providing such desirable residences for sparrows. The sparrows, who appear to nest all the year round, undeterred by fires in the hearths, almost daily hurl down those chimneys straw, feathers and droppings, their nests, their eggs, their piteous naked offspring, and even themselves. It gives the cats a great interest in life, but even they have got a little tired of the daily offering.

Unlike John, I am not good at visualizing alterations. I only know when something is wrong. Now that we actually owned the place, I had to cast off the spell of the chimneys, and look at our future home with open eyes. There seemed to be a good deal wrong.

The house is L-shaped, its gables crow-stepped, but a single-storey Victorian horror had been built on, forming another wing. There was a long, slate-roofed excrescence clinging to the back of the house, blocking a south window. There was an almost Emett-like lavatory perched on top of a porch in the angle of the wall. Some of the mullioned windows had been wrongly restored and had too few lights. Inside the house I did not need to be a visualizer to see that there was no larder, no linen cupboard, an obsolete heating system, and the paint was all an extraordinary mustard colour, which had been slapped on by the army when they evacuated the house in 1945.

At this stage, having adjusted ourselves to the realization that we had bought the Manor, we were seized and possessed by a crusading spirit — we must restore the old house to its ancient glory. John's optimism, and my impatience for perfection, were dangerous horses for beggars to ride, and they more or less bolted with their riders.

2 WE got ourselves an Architect, and the Architect found us the Builder. The Builder, who was a nice man and loved restoring old buildings, was even more optimistic than John and more perfectionist than myself. I think that some of his enthusiasm arose from the fact that the Architect had been so unexpectedly successful in obtaining the permits that were necessary in those days. We had decided that we could afford to spend £500 on alterations and restorations, and we were rather damped when the estimates came to about £1,000. But when the Architect proudly announced that he had got us a permit to spend £1,500, a mad mood of jubilation descended on all of us. Caution and Anxiety flew out of the window, without so much as a backward glance at our Bank balance, and Ambition led us round the house, with the Builder and the Architect, in a positive orgy of planning.

The Builder's men moved into the house in vast numbers. They made themselves very comfortable in a small laundry room in the Victorian annexe. For decoration they hung on the wall a large notice headed 'Factory Act'. They kept themselves warm with a big electric fire, and kept tea brewing all day long in an electric urn. As they also used the latest models in electric appliances to do almost every job, it wasn't very long before we began to get large electricity bills. We began to feel uneasy.

We felt even more uneasy when the first bills arrived from the Builder and were twice as high as we had expected. Polite inquiry elicited the fact that not only had costs risen, but we had, in our more irresponsible moods, ordered various alterations and improvements that were not in the original estimate.

The Builder used to come with the Architect on the days when John and I drove over to inspect progress. He had a habit of walking around with the Architect and addressing remarks to him, in a voice just loud enough for us to overhear, such as,

'That roof will need £500 spending on it in a few years' time.' or 'I don't think that gable-end will last much longer without underpinning.' I am sure he was only trying to be helpful, and perhaps he assumed we were rich, but these remarks made us shudder.

The Builder liked his men to do a job really well. He had no intention of hurrying, and said as much. But we had already turned our cottage over to a new owner, and had been living with various kind friends for some weeks, feeling rather like displaced persons. So at last we decided to move in with the workmen, in the hope of getting them out a little sooner.

We moved into the Manor on a wet November day. It was the thirteenth of the month. I wish I could record that we spent our first evening in front of a roaring wood fire, throwing care to the winds, cracking a bottle of champagne, and crying 'Bless this House'. We did have a roaring wood fire and something to drink. But, exhausted by the strenuous day and depressed by a rather anxious letter from our Bank Manager, we felt more like cursing the house. I recall, to my shame, crouching on the hearth in a terrible fit of homesickness, the tears running down my face, and sobbing inanely to poor John, 'I want to go home to my cottage!'

3 ✤ BUT even a worrier like myself cannot forever remain anxious and miserable — a state my Mrs. Selby calls 'downy'. The workmen had at last been winkled out of their warm room and had reluctantly departed, taking with them the 'Factory Act', the tea-urn and the stove, but leaving in exchange a huge heap of empty cigarette cartons and wrappings from packets of Smith's Crisps. They also left behind a great deal of further necessary work to be done in the future. But with the help of Mrs. Selby, who came round from the farm next door to 'do' for me in the mornings, I was gradually putting the house in order, and it was pleasant to have more room than we had ever enjoyed before.

Contrary to a deep-rooted idea that in East Anglia one is a 'foreigner' and is so treated for at least thirty years, we have found nothing but kindness and friendliness among Suffolk people in every walk of life. We soon found that we were going out and about almost too much. Our son, Jeremy, came down from Oxford for the vacation; some friends came to stay; and quite suddenly we began to feel at home.

A royalty cheque arrived for John. Although it must have been but a drop in the bucket of our overdraft, it was all the encouragement he needed to buy the first yew hedge. We had been lucky to find a jobbing gardener in the shape of Alfred, an endearing character, slow-speaking, simple-hearted and loyal. He and John had cleared the offending Lonicera hedge, and made a start on the sweeping lawn for which Miles yearned. Between this lawn and the paddocks the first yew hedge was planted. Eight dozen bushes required for this hedge cost 42s. a dozen though they were less than two feet high. When spaced out at 24-inch intervals they looked slightly ridiculous.

Since that day I have given John yew bushes for Christmas and birthdays, for anniversary presents, and as Easter Eggs. When feeling 'downy' I have said, 'I shall never live long enough to see those hedges grow to their proper height.' But today many of them are head high. Separate bushes have grown together to make long, solid walls of dark green. They are lovely to see on Autumn mornings, when they are draped with a million cobwebs, each web diamond-studded with a million dewdrops, quivering with light. They are lovely, too, in the Spring, when they turn golden for a week or two as the new shoots appear.

Although comfortably settled — if rather precariously from a financial point of view — John and I still took a keen interest in other people's houses, both empty and occupied. It is an interest we have kept to this day, and we still study the House Agents' advertisements with close attention and enjoyment. Many times a week, one or other of us may be heard to exclaim, 'Ah, now that's a house I wouldn't mind having!'

Three miles away from the Manor is a very handsome Elizabethan mansion, Hemingstone Hall. When we heard one day that the old lady who lived there had died, and the house might be sold, we were naturally interested, because *that* was a house we certainly wouldn't have minded owning! The contents of the Hall were to be sold, and the View Day before the Sale gave us an excellent opportunity to inspect the inside of the house. One look at the vast, old-fashioned kitchen, complete with a huge, rusty range, and great bacon hooks hanging from the cobwebby beams high up above our heads, was enough for me. If it hadn't been, a climb up to the many attics, whose floors were strewn with basins of all shapes and sizes to catch the rain, would have clinched the matter. But, needless to say, John was enthusiastic about the possibilities of the house. 'We could make a lovely place of this,' he said.

'If we had £10,000 to spend on it and were not broke already,' I answered, tartly. 'And do remember we have got a house, and I just couldn't face re-making another garden.' Rather reluctantly John made an effort to see reason.

There were, however, one or two things in the sale of

furniture that interested us, including an old refectory table that would go beautifully in our dining room, and a fireback that would protect the brickwork in the hearth. So we planned to go to the sale next day.

For some reason I was too busy to go with John and our son Jeremy next day. They had gone off in the morning, as the table and one or two other interesting items were to be sold before lunch. I had finished preparing that meal, and had gone into the garden to look at a hedgehog that Alfred had found under a hedge. She lay comfortably on her side in a nest of dead leaves, suckling her six babies as placidly as a cat with kittens. I had just stroked one of the little grunting creatures, its spines as soft as hair, when I heard the car coming down the drive. It was coming rather fast, with the gravel spurting from under the wheels, but as Jeremy was driving there was nothing unusual in that.

I walked round to the front of the house to meet them, wondering if they had been lucky at the sale. Jeremy was beaming, and obviously bursting with news. He could not bear to waste time putting the car away. 'Don't tell her until I'm ready, Dad,' he said.

John looked pleased, but also, I thought a little sheepish. It is, of course, a miracle and a blessing that after so many years of married life we are still sensitive to each other's moods and expressions. But sometimes I feel, on particular occasions, that it is rather bad luck for one or other of us.

Jeremy came running up. 'We got them!' he said.

'Oh good. You got the table and the fireback, then?'

'Oh no Mum, but we. . .'

John put his arm round me. I liked it there, but my heart sank. 'As a matter of fact,' he said, 'somehow we missed the table and. . .'

'But we bought the two peacocks!' cried Jeremy.

'You bought *what*?'

'This is it', we said

But there was a good deal that had to be altered

Araminta

'Actually they are peahens,' said John. 'Now, let's go in and have a drink, and I'll tell you what happened.'

I was led in, dazed and unbelieving, and quite powerless to do anything about lunch. John and Jeremy behaved like two nurses in charge of an important but difficult patient. I was put into the most comfortable armchair in our big oak-beamed living room, with my feet up on a stool. John mixed us all a drink while Jeremy fetched another cushion for my back. After two or three gulps I felt able to say, 'Well, let's have it.'

It seems that when they arrived at Hemingstone Hall the lots we were hoping to buy were not due to come up for sale for some little time, so John and Jeremy decided to have a good look round the garden before going into the marquee on the lawn. Walking round the house, they looked up admiringly at the Dutch gable ends, and there, looking down quizzically at the dealers and the bargain-hunters crowding into the marquee, sat two peahens.

By this time John and Jeremy should have been trying to get into the marquee themselves, but it is my opinion that, intoxicated by talk and thoughts of peacocks, they never went near it.

When the luncheon interval was announced, John approached the auctioneer and asked him what was going to happen to the peahens. 'We have had instructions,' he said, 'to have them shot.'

John and Jeremy were horrified. 'They are not for sale, then?' John said, trying to appear indifferent.

Evidently the auctioneer's professional instincts were stirred. 'Well, Sir, I am sure you can have them for a reasonable bid, *if* you can catch them.'

John offered ten shillings for the two, and they were promptly knocked down to him — Extra Lot No. 279 — on the strict understanding that he would make himself responsible for catching them.

'Well!' I said, 'I might have expected to see a bailiff on our lawn, but never a peacock!'

By this time I had forgotten altogether about the table and the fireback. I was raging at the apparent callousness of the new owner of Hemingstone Hall. I was feeling anxious solicitude for the two peahens, and delight that John had saved their lives and given them a new home.

Over a happy if belated lunch, we decided to call the larger hen Araminta, and the smaller one Arabella. But we still had to catch Extra Lot No. 279.

4 ❀ ALFRED works for us two days a week, and although it usually seems to be wet on the days when he is here he arrived with a fine morning the day after the sale. He and John and Jeremy immediately started to build a spacious wire pen, attached to an open shed on the far side of the orchard.

We knew nothing about keeping peafowl, but instinct told us that we should have to keep Araminta and Arabella under restraint for a week or so before giving them the freedom of the garden. Indeed, it is simply instinct and observation that have taught us all we know about them today. I know of only one book on the subject, and that has merely confirmed our observations rather than taught us anything new. Strangely, I have met enthusiastic breeders of these birds whose ideas and theories bear no relation to fact or observation, but still lie in the realms of myth and old wives' tales.

The pen being completed by mid-morning, Jeremy and Alfred set off for Hemingstone Hall after lunch, taking with them in the car a loaf of bread — the bait — and two sacks. I did not expect to see them for a long time. Although the old butler had stayed on at the Hall for a little while after the death of his mistress, he had been gone for some weeks, and I knew that Araminta and Arabella must be growing very wild.

So I was surprised when, about three o'clock, I heard the car coming down the drive, very slowly this time. As John and I went out to meet it, Alfred got out, a huge grin on his face. In his slow, deliberate voice, he said, 'We've got one, Ma'am!'

On the back seat of the car was one of the sacks, bulging, but rather unnaturally still, I thought. John lifted it out very carefully and carried it up to the pen, with Jeremy, Alfred and me trailing after him. Shutting the gate behind him, John laid the sack gently on the ground and opened the neck. It was an exciting moment for me, who had never before seen a peahen except in a zoo. But nothing happened. John cautiously pulled the sack down further. We had rather expected a furious, kicking bird, but Araminta was feeling faint. It had all been too much for her. She lay on her side, breathing very quickly, her beak half open, her eyes shut and her coronet awry. It was not until John gently pulled the sack right off her that she felt able to open her beautiful dark eyes. She struggled to her feet, gave herself a violent shake and retired to a corner of the pen to rest and rearrange her sadly ruffled plumage.

Although some people consider peahens dull to look at, in comparison with the cock, Araminta was beautiful in our eyes. She was a big bird, with soft grey plumage and an exceptionally long green neck, and the white 'kid' on her face was faintly tinged with yellow. But her eyes were her best feature.

We learned from Jeremy and Alfred that, after a few preliminary attempts at catching Araminta while she was eating some bread, they had cornered her in a ruined belvedere. She had tried to fly through a window, cutting her legs slightly. But this healed very quickly, and she settled down well. She didn't seem to mind being penned up, and was very soon taking pieces of digestive biscuit out of our hands. To peafowl, cheese — particularly a nice stale Cheddar — is the greatest treat, but digestive biscuits run it a close second.

Araminta was always a gentle, friendly bird, which probably explained her comparatively easy capture. The capture of her sister, Arabella, was a very different matter, and took a fortnight of varying strategy and tactics.

5 ❧ ARABELLA was a high-flyer. As soon as we appeared in the garden at the back of Hemingstone Hall, where she was usually to be found, she would immediately fly up on to the roof of the house. Even when we stalked her round the corners of out-buildings, concealed ourselves on the roof of the coach-house or crawled through beds of stinging nettles, she somehow sensed our presence and was off before we had a chance to throw down any food.

At this time the Hall was empty and the new owner had put it up for sale. We had an Order to View, and we viewed it pretty thoroughly. Not wanting to bother anyone by continually asking for the key, we effected an entrance, with the aid of an old chair, through a kitchen window at the back. Thus when Arabella took to the air Jeremy would get in through the window, run up to the attics and out on to the roof, creep along the parapet and drive her down again. For this operation he would wear gym shoes, and blacken his face, commando-fashion. The gym shoes seemed sensible, but I never quite understood the blackened face, especially in the daytime. However, he enjoyed himself.

During the Arabella campaign we had an old friend staying with us — Robert Gibbings, the writer and wood-engraver. He was as interested as we were in old houses, and very much wanted to see the inside of Hemingstone Hall. Robert was well over six feet tall and weighed about seventeen stone at that time. I felt a little dubious about the strength of the chair, and the size of the window. However, with a certain amount of pushing and pulling we got him in, more or less unharmed. Getting him out was another matter. He became wedged, straddled across the window sill with one leg inside and one leg out. We pushed and we pulled, but it seemed hopeless. We tried not to hear his cries of pain, intermixed with oaths, all in a rich Irish brogue. At last a concerted effort on the recalcitrant leg did the trick and he tumbled out. But he was not pleased,

21

and claimed that a particularly tender portion of his anatomy had suffered irreparable damage.

It was Robert who suggested setting snares for Arabella — an accomplishment no doubt learnt from his poacher friends — and I think it was I who thought of baiting them with raisins soaked in rum. We duly soaked the raisins, put them in a basin and set off in the car. On the way we felt we ought to try one to see if it was good enough for Arabella. We tried one. It was delicious. We tried several more. When we arrived at the Hall there were only three left. The car was full of rum fumes, and we felt very cheerful. Robert set a snare and we ceremoniously put the three raisins in it. Alas, Arabella evidently did not care for rum. We rather grudged those three wasted raisins.

Arabella put up a long and gallant resistance. In the end hunger defeated her. One day she did not fly up as soon as we appeared. We had fixed a large net in a semi-circle and, walking behind her and throwing bread ahead of her, we slowly drove her into it. The second half of Extra Lot No. 279 was in the bag.

6 BY the time we caught Arabella her sister had been shut up for about two weeks. As they were so obviously pleased to be together again, and as Araminta was such a quiet, sensible bird, we let them both out a few days later. It is nearly impossible to make every hedge and fence secure around three acres, and, if they chose to fly there was nothing we could do about it. So the first few hours after the two birds were set free were nerve-wracking ones for us. But we needn't have worried. At no time did Araminta or Arabella make any attempt to leave our grounds. Having walked rapidly all round and inspected everything thoroughly, they were quite content to stay within the boundaries. Unless they were hunting insects in one of the paddocks they were generally to be found near the house. They liked to perch on a wall within earshot of the kitchen door. When they heard it open they would fly down and rush to the porch in the hope of getting a tit-bit of cheese, some cake crumbs or a digestive biscuit. In the summer, when there are plenty of insects about, our birds are apt to turn up their beaks at their staple diet of cracked maize and wheat.

It was Araminta and Arabella who unhesitatingly chose the oak tree in front of the house as the roosting place. Since then we have had several new, unrelated birds, but they have always gone straight to the oak tree to choose their individual bed-rooms, although they may change these — going on to higher or lower branches — according to the direction of the wind or their own whims. They roost in the tree in all weather, and will never voluntarily take shelter under any roof.

One day, as we stood indulging our time-wasting occupation of gazing admiringly at our peahens, John said, 'What a pity they haven't got a man in their lives.'

'We have no idea how old they are,' I said, 'they may be too old for that sort of thing. And we can't afford a peacock.'

'Arabella had laid some eggs just before we caught her,' said

23

John, adding: 'And think what we saved by getting them so cheaply!'

Soon after this conversation we went to a cocktail party, and one of the guests told us of someone in Hertfordshire who bred peafowl. As we often went back to Hertfordshire to visit friends it seemed worth while just making an enquiry. A telephone call told us that a Miss Page-May had a young peacock, just turned two, that she felt she must sell as he was beginning to fight with his father.

On our way to a weekend visit we called in at Much Hadham to have a look at the peacock, purely out of interest. Miss Page-May had a lot of land, and we had quite a walk before we found the family. They were deep in some long grass, and all that could be seen of them at first were their little crowned heads, white kid faces and bright eyes peering up at us. Miss Page-May called to them and they came slowly towards us. I don't think either of us will ever forget the shock of pleasure we experienced at our first sight of the young peacock — that brilliant blue neck and breast emerging from the green grass. He led the way, as befitted the man of the family — his father was not around. His coronet was a shimmering blue, his 'kid' was snowy white and his eyes were large, brown, liquid and bold. He lifted his feet high, walking slowly, deliberately and proudly.

'We will call him "Lucifer",' said John.

So that was that.

We arranged to collect Lucifer on our way home. Miss Page-May hoped to catch him in her morning-room, which he often visited. This she did, and when we arrived on the Monday he was in a very different condition from the bird we had seen two days before. Poor fellow. It reminded me of the lines, 'How art thou fallen from Heaven, O Lucifer, son of the morning!'

He had not yet grown a full-length tail — in any case all

peacocks moult their long tails by the end of July — and he was stuffed into the sort of basket in which plumbers carry their tools, with the handles tied together over his back. His head and neck stuck out at one end, and his black tail feathers at the other. All he could move were his eyes, and he eyed us with fury.

The bridegroom's departure for the home of his brides was not exactly a triumphal one. Lucifer was humbled; we were anxious about getting him home unharmed; Miss Page-May hated losing him and was nearly in tears; and her land-girl, who had fed him from a chick, was weeping openly.

7 ※ ALTHOUGH Lucifer was already a tame bird when
we bought him, he still had to endure a period in the
pen, so that he could get to know us and accustom
himself to new surroundings. His wives did their best to amuse
him during this dreary time. They would spend long hours
sitting on a pile of logs close to the pen, preening their feathers.
Or, combining business with pleasure, they would take energetic dust baths on a nearby rubbish heap — a somewhat
ludicrous sight as they scratched, burrowed and rolled.

Araminta was always Lucifer's favourite. Even at this time
she and Lucifer might be seen with their beaks as close together
as the wire permitted, their heads nearly touching the ground.
Peafowl will stand in this position, without moving, for minutes
at a time. Perhaps one will then very gently nibble the other's
'kid'. That this gesture indicates affection is certain, but I
suppose it is possible that they may also be pecking at small
verminous insects. We call this rather touching habit 'being in
conference'. A peacock will 'confer' in this manner with his
wives, and with his daughters, but never with another cock. A
peahen will confer with any of her children up to the moment
— which comes at the beginning of the next breeding season —
when she casts them off, and will suddenly drive them from
her almost savagely. Although by this time they are probably
larger than their mother, their bewilderment at this sudden
volte face is pathetic.

Unlike his wives, Lucifer did cause us a certain amount of
anxiety when he was first let out of the pen. At times he seemed
more interested in the poultry in the neighbouring stack-yard
than in Araminta and Arabella, and he was clever at finding
places in the hedge where he could slip through to fraternise
with his hen friends.

Although, luckily, it doesn't seem to occur to them to fly far
unless frightened, some peafowl are great walkers, and until
they are thoroughly familiar with their environment they can

be very stupid at finding their way home. So we had to be continually on the alert during Lucifer's first weeks of freedom. Little work was done in the house or garden, or at the desk. Whoever discovered that Lucifer was missing would blow the beagling horn — a useful instrument of unknown origin, no doubt acquired at some sale along with the umbrella stand and the hip-bath — and off we would go in pursuit.

Lucifer was usually quite near home, and often seemed relieved to be fetched back. Sometimes, indeed, he found his own way back along the road, and could be seen outside the front gates patiently waiting for someone to let him in. By the time we had secured every possible means of exit in fences and hedges, Lucifer discovered that nothing was easier or more enjoyable than to fly up on to one of the brick gate piers and survey the world from there, jumping down on to the road when bored with the prospect. These excursions outside our property could also be made by way of the brick wall that formed the boundary between ourselves and our neighbours the Selbys. He enjoyed a walk among their cows until the moment when one, more curious than the rest, would advance upon him, and then he would come flying home, uttering screams.

Many peafowl are afraid of wire, and a single strand fixed a foot above a wall or hedge will usually prevent them from flying over. So we had to get busy fixing up wire everywhere. The gate piers, with stone balls on top, were rather a problem, but we managed to contrive a Heath-Robinson-like affair of wire and sticks which seemed to deter Lucifer temporarily. Soon our garden had the appearance of a prison or a concentration camp. For that matter, it still has, though after a while we gave up worrying about Lucifer's wanderings. He is most restless when he has lost his long train in the midsummer moult, and his wives are busy with those boring chicks. He used to pay frequent visits to the church, about a quarter of a mile down the lane — evidently the grass and insects in the church-yard were more appetizing than ours. At first we worried about the possibility of a car hitting him, but he always returned safely, and we ceased to worry.

Unfortunately Lucifer formed the habit of visiting one of the cottage gardens on his way home, to enjoy a refreshing lettuce. This made him unpopular there, and after this was reported to us, we felt in duty bound to go after him again. To drive a peacock who does not wish to be driven is a nightmare. They are the friendliest of creatures, and take food gently and courteously from one's hand. But they are quite unafraid of human beings, and resent taking marching orders. In fact they cannot be driven, unless one is carrying a long, thin stick. We hadn't yet learnt to keep several long, thin sticks in strategic positions.

Having somehow got Lucifer out of the cottage garden and onto the road he might follow me for a few steps. But then he would stop on the grass verge for a very leisurely meal of grass and insects. At any attempt to hustle him, he would give me an outraged look and slip through a hole in the hedge into a corn-field. I would laboriously climb the gate into the field, seizing a short stick out of the hedge. A flourish with this would some-times startle him sufficiently to make him hop back into the road. But as soon as he realized it was only a short stick he took no notice of it at all. I would advance on him waving it, and he would merely turn round, rise to his full height, his large brown eyes flashing contemptuously, and refuse to budge at all. All I could do was to abandon him and hope for the best, or to go on ahead, calling him in a voice that suggested digestive biscuits. If we were near home, and he thought that his wives and children might be going to get them first, he would con-descend to follow me. I would arrive home hot, hoarse and cross, and temporarily cursing all peafowl.

One day a lorry very nearly hit Lucifer, and he flew, screaming, to the top of a very high elm tree, where he remained for two hours. This adventure rather put him off his visits to the church, and he does not wander far nowadays. A visit to the Selbys is about the limit of his excursions. He used to spend long hours gazing at his reflection in the glass windows of their hen houses, but last year, in the course of some restorations, we provided him with a french window on home territory, and now he much prefers this.

I have no explanation of the fact that Lucifer will retreat at the sight of a long, thin stick. It may be that it evokes the idea of a snake in his tiny subconscious mind. But this is only a tentative theory and I have no proof that it is correct.

8 ❧ THE time passed quickly and pleasantly. We were doing some more work on the house — rebuilding the old back porch which we had left unfinished in our anxiety to get rid of the workmen. This was an interesting job as it called for a certain amount of detective work. Although it was clear that there had always been a porch there, marks on the outside wall indicated that at some time the top had been a different shape. Internally and externally the house had been altered surprisingly little. We mourned the loss of panelling from some of the rooms; we could not decide the exact position of the original staircase or where the ladder must, in the old days, have led up to the attic floor, and we can never be sure that we have restored the back porch correctly. But once we had opened up the old fireplaces and removed the Victorian excrescence from the south side, we could see both the internal and external plan of the house without difficulty. It is still possible to see where the original front porch — probably built of stone — led into the house.

We were still altering and improving the garden, and digging out part of the old moat, which proved to be a storehouse of relics. We found many pieces of pottery dating from the fifteenth to the eighteenth centuries; several of the original leaded windows from the house, and a large quantity of carved and worked stone of all sizes. Some of the smaller pieces had once been painted, and we thought it almost certain that they had formed part of the original front porch. Two massive pieces were carved with the letter 'S', a reminder that the house was built by John Southwell about 1550.

By now the peafowl had become thoroughly established. Towards the end of April Araminta and Arabella were to be seen wandering in the paddocks and along hedges and ditches, looking for suitable nesting places. 'Nest' is perhaps a rather grandiose term for the shallow hole the peahen scoops out of the ground, and 'suitable' does not describe some of the places they decided upon as a first choice.

One such place was in a herbaceous border, which meant that it could not be weeded for more than six weeks. There have been other unfortunate places, such as the one just by the wood pile, where a dislodged log could have crushed the hen, her eggs or both. The nature of the nest makes both the hen and the eggs vulnerable to attack from rats, birds of prey, foxes and, alas, humans, too.

By this time Lucifer was in all his feathered glory. His train was nearly 1½ yards long, and the beauty of its colours was indescribable. When he raised it and spread it, while courting, it made a halo of shimmering lights all around him — blue, mauve and different greens. In the sunlight the whole feathered arc looked as though it were sprinkled with gold dust.

When very excited he would stamp and paw the ground, often walking backwards towards the object of his affection. He could agitate his black under-feathers to make a strange and unearthly noise — something like the rustle of dead leaves shivering in a high wind.

As a matter of fact, the sheer mechanics of this display are as marvellous as its aesthetic appeal. This beautiful fan is not a true tail. All its feathers — there are around fifty, each quill with a single 'eye' — grow from the peacock's back, and they are supported by the stiff, short, black feathers of his true tail which grows underneath his train. Round his rump and below his true tail grow some very soft downy feathers, which always remind me of the feather boa my mother used to wear when I was a child. I must admit here that the back view of Lucifer's display always strikes me as slightly ridiculous.

Although, of course, the adult bird does his displaying during the mating season, I do not think it is invariably a sign of sexual virility. I have seen many a three-week-old chick fan out its diminutive tail and strut about just like its father. Peacocks will, in fact, display before all sorts of objects as well as their wives — ducks, sparrows, even a lawn mower. When we want Lucifer to show off before guests, we can usually make him display by merely throwing down a handful of maize in front of him. Sometimes he will even try to bend and eat it with his fan fully spread.

Hen birds will often raise and fan out their short tails, paw the ground and stamp in exactly the same manner as the peacock. There never seems much reason for this, although I think they sometimes do it when they are feeling belligerent. I have seen our hens 'display' like this preparatory to jumping angrily on one of our cats that has dared to go too close. These varying display rituals have baffled ornithologists throughout the ages, and will no doubt continue to do so. About one thing there can be no dispute: the fantastic beauty of it all.

Courtship

A face at the window

9 ❦ TOWARDS the end of May we noticed that Araminta and Arabella would disappear for several hours every day. We guessed that at last they must have settled on nesting places. We watched them carefully when they were with us, but they were coy, secretive and much too clever. We never saw where they went.

When Alfred finds something in the garden which he thinks may interest us — it may be anything from a dead mole to a fragment of Elizabethan pottery he has dug up — he solemnly comes to John and says in his slow drawl, 'I've got something to show you, Sir!' So when he produced this opening gambit one morning we guessed what he had found.

We followed him out, Alfred on tip-toe, a huge smile spread across his face. He led us to the far side of the paddock, and there, under a hedge, was a scooped-out hollow in the grass with four eggs in it.

The prospect of actually breeding peafowl had, until that moment, always seemed a little remote. We gazed at the nest with awe. The colour of the eggs was similar to that of domestic hens' eggs, and although they were larger, they were not as big as we had expected, considering that both the hens were big birds.

This triumph of detective work put Alfred on his mettle, and it wasn't long before he led us up to another nest under an oak tree in the middle of the smaller paddock. This contained five eggs. In all the years since those first exciting moments it has always been Alfred who has found the nests first.

When the peahens have started sitting in earnest it is easy to find which bird is sitting on which nest. Once a day — occasionally only once every two days — the hen will get off her eggs, take to her wings and fly towards the house, cackling loudly and wildly at the same time. Sometimes if the wind is strong or she has taken off at the wrong angle she may land far from her objective. We have had to fetch hens back from the

Selby's meadow and the neighbouring stack-yard, and the possibility of this occurrence has caused us anxiety when we have had to be away from home.

The hens expect to find food and water awaiting them near the house, and will strut round, neck outstretched and feathers ruffled, honking loudly at intervals, until this is provided. They then peck wildly and jerkily at the food, snatch a drink of water, and generally seem *distrait* and restless.

'Ah, she be whully proud on her eggs!' Mrs. Selby will say, on witnessing this behaviour. She may be right, but it is a fact that peafowl tend to be hysterical at times, and I think the excitement is due not so much to maternal pride as to maternal agitation.

After this sketchy meal the hen may take time off for a dust bath, if the weather is fine and the soil dry. The place chosen for this part of her toilet is often a flower border, where her energetic scratching and rolling will break down several delphiniums which are just coming into bloom or plough up a patch where seeds have been sown. After about ten minutes the hen returns to her nest, usually by some devious route, and much more quietly than when she left it.

A peahen sits for a full twenty-eight days, and when our two were sitting for the first time we felt a mounting excitement and tension towards the end of this period. We did not know how many eggs would hatch, what the chicks would look like, or what sort of mothers Araminta and Arabella would make.

I was in the kitchen one morning at the end of June, getting breakfast, when I heard John give a great shout. Dropping an egg into the sink I rushed and joined him at the dining-room window. Walking slowly down the Long Walk, stepping high and deliberately, was Araminta. Clustered round her legs, so close that it seemed impossible that she could avoid stepping on them, were four tiny brown and yellow chicks.

We went out of the porch door and cautiously approached

34

the little family. We needn't have worried. Araminta always trusted us completely and she didn't, like so many hens, either walk the chicks rapidly away or immediately sit down and brood them. Indeed, she seemed 'whully proud' of them. They were smaller than we had expected, and at that stage very closely resembled the chicks of a domestic hen. To us, they were the prettiest little things we had ever seen. Araminta was already looking for insects, which she tried to feed to the chicks from her beak, but they eat very little for twenty-four hours, and she soon settled down to brood them.

Araminta had laid five eggs, so we looked in the nest to make sure that a chick had not been left behind. But, as is so often the case, one egg was obviously infertile. However, we were quite satisfied with four lovely chicks, and I went happily back to the kitchen, which I found dense with the smoke from burnt and blackened toast.

10❧ OUR first intimation of Arabella's motherhood was the sight of her walking across the paddock, a few days later, with one solitary chick in attendance. She was pecking it vigorously. We hurried to her nest and saw that four out of her five eggs had hatched. But there was no sign of the other chicks.

We made a quick search and discovered one chick in a ditch, caught up in some brambles, and two struggling feebly in long grass in the paddock. We collected them and took them to Arabella who by now had reached the lawn. She was still pecking at her exhausted chick, who was longing to rest and be brooded. As Arabella felt rather tired herself she did condescend to sit down for a moment, and we tried to put the three other chicks under her. But it was hopeless. Arabella had no intention of being a good mother. She got up again, and started pecking at all the chicks indiscriminately.

There was only one thing to do. We had to try and find a broody domestic hen, a coop and a wire run, as quickly as possible. While John sent out an S.O.S. to friends and neighbours, I put the four chicks in a basket and set it down by the kitchen boiler.

While John was doing the organizing, I spent what was left of the day brooding peachicks. The warmth soon revived them, and in half-an-hour they were out of the basket, pattering over the kitchen floor and chirruping cheerfully. They quickly adopted me as a foster-mother, and in no time they discovered that they could be comfortably 'brooded' if they climbed up on my shoes and got inside the legs of my slacks. I spent some difficult hours trying to cook, with two peachicks up each trouser leg. When rested they would pop down and roam round the kitchen floor, pecking uselessly at anything I might have dropped. I loved them dearly.

Eventually the Selbys found a broody hen, and some other kind neighbours appeared with a hen-coop. John quickly knocked up a wire run. That night after dark we put the chicks under the hen. She grumbled and pecked as broody hens do, but she gathered the chicks under her wings quite contentedly and we went to bed feeling reasonably happy about them.

11 ❧ WE had several disappointing seasons while we were learning how to cope with the peafowl, their diseases and their vagaries. But perhaps this first breeding season was the saddest, because we hadn't foreseen the difficulties or learnt, as we did later, to be philosophical about them. We were utterly miserable every time a peachick died, and out of this first year's batch there was only one survivor.

We had such a lot to learn, and only time and experience could teach us. We did not know, for instance, that peachicks are prey to every disease that attacks ordinary chicks and turkey poults, and that they are even more delicate than the latter. Even if we had realized this we shouldn't at that time have known what to do about it.

We didn't realize that the previous owner of the Manor had kept poultry and that, therefore, the ground was bound to be infected with Coccidiosis and Blackhead, the two great killer diseases, and we didn't know that these germs could be carried by birds of the air from the farms on either side of us. Again, even if we had known these facts, ignorance would have prevented us from doing anything about it.

For several years I had to experiment with antibiotics, both as preventives, and in the treatment of a particular disease. I had to learn at what age the chicks were liable to contract any of the likely diseases. With peafowl by far the most satisfactory method of preventing disease is to doctor their drinking water with different antibiotics at different times. But while this is easy in the case of penned birds such as turkeys, it is much more difficult to manage with peafowl who are roaming freely. They much prefer to drink out of a puddle if it has recently rained.

It is only in the last three or four years that we have managed to rear all the chicks that have been hatched, and even now a long spell of rain causes us anxiety. While the chicks are small

38

there are also the hazards of attack by birds of prey, rats and, although I hesitate to say it, our own cats. It is only when the chicks reach the age of seven or eight months that we feel we can relax, and even then we have to watch for signs of illness so that we can, in good time, push an antibiotic capsule down their protesting throats.

Disease and ignorance combined to beat us that first sad season, which had appeared to start so auspiciously with the arrival of Araminta's chicks. All went well for the first few weeks. It was just at the time when their little coronets first appeared as tiny black dots on their heads that Araminta's chicks, one by one, started to sicken and die. We began to be familiar with the horrid pattern. The chick would go off its food, lag behind the others and then try and catch up with hurried runs, and, in some subtle way that it is impossible to describe, its shape would change. Its shoulders would become hunched; it hung its head. In two days it would be dead.

Of Arabella's abandoned family none survived, in spite of the devotion of their foster-mother. I realize now, of course that we shouldn't have kept them so confined to their pen. We did this because Arabella, having nothing to do but swan around looking for trouble, was always ready to advance and give them all a good peck when they were let out, and the hen was unable to protect them as a peahen mother would have done. But this confinement meant that they were not getting nearly enough natural food in the shape of insects of all sorts, and the various kinds of grasses and seeds. They were not very keen on the chick-meal mash I was feeding to them. I think it is doubtful, though, whether freedom would have made much difference in the end.

Araminta was eventually left with one chick, a young pea-hen. This was odd, as the hens are usually the more delicate birds. But Clarissa, as we named this sole survivor, appeared to thrive.

We gradually forgot our disappointment over the other misfortunes in our pride in Clarissa. She was a delightful little bird. She became very tame, like her mother, and was soon eating out of our hands. We never tired of watching her. When we called her she would come running across the lawn, her neck stretched, her dappled breast thrust forward, and her long legs flashing. She was always full of enthusiasm and *joie de vivre*.

When we had our tea out of doors Araminta and Clarissa, as though informed by some sixth sense, would soon be standing by our deck chairs, waiting for digestive biscuits. In another few minutes Lucifer would arrive, followed by that unnatural mother, Arabella. This family gathering used to amuse and delight our visitors.

12 ✿ ALTHOUGH the parish church of St. Mary stands in our lane, we have no village and are rather a scattered parish. Long ago there must have been a village, but after the ravages of the Black Death in the seventeenth century many of the old stud-and-plaster houses were deliberately burnt down, while brick-built houses such as ours escaped. So, apart from the Selbys, we have no neighbours we can visit without getting into the car, and friends have to use a car to visit us. This means that there is not much of the casual popping in and out one gets in village life. If a journey is not to be wasted it is safer to telephone first. But friends whose occasions often take them down our lane do drop in for coffee or a drink, and to see the peafowl.

Frequent and welcome visitors during our early years here were the 'Squarson' of a neighbouring parish and his wife. Many people are amused by the term 'Squarson', or ignorant of it. It goes back in time to the days when many parsons had independent incomes and were the squires as well as the rectors of their people. They probably spent as much time hunting and shooting as they did officiating in church, but many a parishioner would find a brace of pheasants or a basket of fruit on his doorstep. The Squarson took care of their bodies as well as their souls.

Although I am sure he did not have the sort of income enjoyed by Squarsons of bygone days, our somewhat idiosyncratic friend Algernon tried to live as far as possible in the old tradition. He never wore a dog-collar, and it wasn't until our second meeting, at a summer party in a gnat-infested garden, that we realized who he was. We had heard that he was eccentric. I realized he wasn't quite the usual kind of parson when his reply to my query, made by way of conversation, as to whether my forehead had been bitten by the gnats, was 'It's nothing a kiss wouldn't cure.'

Algernon and his wife Elsie lived in a Queen Anne rectory

standing splendidly in parkland. The house was very beautiful, but icy cold in winter, during which time they would abandon the graciously proportioned reception rooms and retire to a small, snug, low room in the Tudor part of the house. Not even a Squarson could afford to feed the vast and obsolete boiler that once worked the central heating. Anyway, it would probably have blown up.

The house was large and the garden larger. There was a magnificent tulip tree, and a very beautiful orangery in which we often sat eating Elsie's delicious cucumber sandwiches while admiring the tree. There were also acres of walled-gardens. Algernon and Elsie managed most of it single-handed, and although they could not keep it as it must have once been kept, they grew every sort of flower, fruit, vegetable and berry. I have never understood how they managed it, just as I have never understood how Elsie managed the large house — which was always in a spotless condition — as well as fulfilling her numerous parish duties. She also had to be a more than average cook, because Algernon loved good food.

One of Algernon's hobbies was brewing home-made wine in his vast cellars. Once when we were dining at the rectory we were given parsnip wine as an *aperitif,* dandelion wine with the fish, rhubarb wine with the meat, and marigold brandy as a *liqueur.* They all tasted delicious, but they didn't really suit our digestions. We had a restless night.

Algernon drove a very ancient Rolls Royce — a two-seater with a dickey. It was a familiar sight, lumbering along our lanes with Algernon's rather stout figure perched aloft in the high cab, as if enthroned. He was the most generous of men, and the dickey was usually full of presents for his friends. He and Elsie rarely came to see us without bringing some gift — flowers, tomatoes, a basket of peaches, or some game he had shot. He was a keen collector of edible fungi, and would some-times arrive with a gigantic puff-ball. He insisted these were delicious when cooked, but we never grew to like them very much.

Algernon had unexpected tastes. Although so devoted to shootin' and fishin' he was also one of the few people we have known who shared our pleasure in the somewhat esoteric novels of T. F. Powys. He would read and re-read them, but confessed that he had always disliked pigs after reading *Mr. Tasker's Gods*. He and Elsie had a great interest in the arts generally, and he was constantly returning from Cambridge, Ipswich or Bury St. Edmund's with some pieces of porcelain or an obscure eighteenth-century print that he had discovered in a back-street junk shop.

His parishioners loved their Squarson in spite of, or perhaps because of, his eccentricities. He treated everyone with old-fashioned courtesy. I know that many a sick or lonely woman was the happier for a visit from him. He would not only take them something delicious to tempt their appetites, but would boost their morale with well-chosen and graciously delivered compliments. It was a sad day for all of us when Algernon was appointed an Archdeacon, and he and Elsie moved away to a Cathedral city.

13 ❀ THE comparative calm of this period was rudely shattered one day by a letter from our Bank Manager. Perhaps 'rudely' is not the right word, because our Bank Manager is a kindly man, considerate, courteous and sympathetic. We have always told him every detail of our financial lives — our hopes, fears and expectations, if any. He has appreciated this, I think. But this was the time of a governmental Credit Squeeze, and a higher authority than he had decided that our overdraft must be reduced. We hadn't quite realized how large this had become.

We did a little simple arithmetic. The results showed us that we were earning the bread and butter of life, but not the jam that we were inclined to spread rather liberally. We did further sums. Once the jam was spread, it seemed impossible to scrape off enough to make any difference to our situation.

The weather at this time was fine and warm, and the sunshine had that golden mellowness that comes with early Autumn. By now the moat which we had cleared and dug out had filled up to the brim, and the water lay quiet and still, reflecting the skimming swallows and the tall old willow that was thriving now that its roots were in water. Many small birds — mainly various kinds of warblers — flitted and twitted among the branches and greeny-grey leaves, sometimes sending a dead leaf twisting down to the water.

But we were feeling rather more than 'downy'. We were despondent and apprehensive, and could take little pleasure in these things. In fact the growing beauty of the place made us feel worse because, although neither of us said a word, we both knew what the other was thinking. We knew we ought to look for a cheaper house and try to recoup some of our losses. We went about our jobs with heavy hearts, and we could hardly look the peafowl in the eye. It didn't help us to realize that John's optimism and my impatience were the chief causes of our plight.

44

We were sitting by the moat one day, having our 'elevenses' and passing pieces of biscuit to Lucifer, who was standing between us, when John, braver than I, said the fatal words: 'We can't afford to go on living here, you know.'

Although I may have lived with it for some time, when I am presented with an unpalatable fact I cannot face up to it on the spot. I like to go away and study it in private. I do not know if this is cowardice, stupidity, or an over-developed sense of privacy. Anyhow, I stalled.

'It's getting a bit late in the year to try and sell a house,' I said. 'People like to buy houses in the Spring, not the Autumn. And how can we afford to sell it when we've spent so much money on it that we shall never see again? Couldn't we hang on until next Spring, and then see how your next book sells?'

These delaying tactics, I realized at the time, originated in a Micawber-like feeling, common to both of us, that Something might turn up. Something usually had turned up, and no doubt this had had a weakening effect on our characters.

A week or two later Something did turn up.

For some weeks past we had noticed a blue Ford car standing outside our gates for quite long periods, the woman driver sitting at the wheel and gazing down the drive. 'Is it the house or the peafowl that attracts her?' we wondered.

On this particular day she got out of the car and walked up the drive towards the house. She was a grey-haired, middle-aged woman, dressed in tweeds and wearing what is known as 'sensible' shoes. She was voluble in her apologies for intruding. Her accent told us at once that she was an American. Her name, she told us, was Miss Boult and she came from California.

She said she simply adored our house and indeed had wanted to buy it when it was in the market, but we had made an offer first. Could she possibly walk round the garden?

We let her walk round the garden and round the house as well, pointing out with pride the alterations and improvements

45

we had made to both. By now forgetful of our current financial crisis, we outlined all the plans we were making for future improvements.

Miss Boult bubbled over with enthusiasm and appreciation. We all agreed that nothing was too good for a house as beautiful as this. While we were sitting over coffee we told her of our plans to restore, one by one, the leaded lights in the windows. Her remark that it would be worth it, even if one were being carried out in one's coffin while the last window was being fixed, endeared her to us.

We ought to have felt incredulous relief, but all we felt was a sense of shock and outrage, when Miss Boult suddenly asked if there was any possibility that we might sell the house to her. We did not know what to say. John and I looked at each other anxiously. We hummed and hawed. We explained that we had spent so much on the house that only a big offer could tempt us. Miss Boult said she thought she would be able to make a big offer. Might she do so?

It was obvious that if the offer were big enough it was our plain duty to consider it. So, feeling — quite illogically — much less friendly to Miss Boult, we asked her to communicate with us through an Estate Agent, and washed our hands of any further personal contact with her.

In due course the Agent sent us her offer. It was big enough to ensure that we recovered most of what we had spent on the house, and it was, we were sure, far more than we should have got in the open market at that time. We asked the Agent to make it clear to Miss Boult that we could not accept the offer until we had found somewhere else to live, and we swore them both to secrecy as we did not want to upset Mrs. Selby and Alfred before it was necessary.

Once again we were house-hunting.

14 ❦ THIS was an unhappy time of tension and conflict. Even our usual enjoyment in viewing other people's houses deserted us. We had lived long enough at the Manor to love every brick, beam and cobweb, and we had so many plans for its future. We liked our neighbours and all the friends we had made. My conservatism made me hate the idea that we should have to leave Mrs. Selby and Alfred, to change our doctor, and even our Garage, where they knew the foibles of our old car so well. Poor John! I am afraid that I was cantankerous and difficult.

If it had been difficult to find a house to suit us some years ago, it seemed quite hopeless now. We had been spoilt. And we just could not bring ourselves to abandon the peafowl. When we inspected a property it had to be judged from their viewpoint! Was there enough land for them, and was it far enough from other houses to ensure that the inhabitants were not disturbed by Lucifer's uninhibited Spring-time shrieks? Of course, the house had to be old and attractive, and have modern conveniences, and not require any money spending on it.

The only house that would have suited the peafowl did not suit me. Although John, with his optimism and imagination, would have settled for it — it had an octagonal drawing room and certain other obscure points of architectural interest — I think that with the experiences of recent winters behind us we did well not to let ourselves in for the half mile of private road down which no snow plough would have appeared, the mile walk to fetch the milk, and the vast, unheated kitchen. Undoubtedly the peafowl would have loved its isolation and the large unmown paddocks. They could have perched on the ruined and collapsing stables, and screamed themselves hoarse without annoying anyone. I could see the place had its advantages. But I just couldn't face the disadvantages.

Always, when we returned to the Manor, tired and dispirited after each fruitless search round the countryside, we would look down the drive at the house for a moment before going in, and we would both say, 'We haven't yet seen anything as beautiful as this, and we never shall.'

The time came when Miss Boult, who had really been very patient, wanted an answer before returning to America. After a long and exhausting conference, we decided that as we quite obviously hadn't found anywhere else to live we must, willynilly, have some faith in the future, try to cut down expenses, and go on living at the Manor for the time being. We informed the agent accordingly, and said we would let him know if we ever found another house.

It is no good trying to keep secrets in the country. One day, in our absence, Miss Boult had sent a builder to the Manor to estimate for some possible alterations. On our return home we found Mrs. Selby in tears. 'Oh dear-O,' she said. 'You've spent all that money on the housen and now you're leaving! Well, dew you go, I 'ont work for anyone else, that I 'ont. Oh dear-o, I dew feel downy!'

We dried her tears, gave her a glass of sherry, and told her the whole story. We said that we were not going to sell the house — not at present anyway. Being able to reassure Mrs. Selby gave us the only happy moments we had had for weeks.

John was working on three books at once

Not for Sale

15 ❧ HAVING decided not to sell the house, we tried to relax a little and not to worry too much. As a matter of fact, there wasn't much time for brooding, because we both put our noses to the grindstone in a renewed if rather vain effort to work off some of our overdraft. John was working on three books at once, and I was trying to write short stories. Expenses had to be cut as well as more money earned, and all the hard work had to be done on one small drink in the evening and no wine with our meals; though John wasted a certain amount of his mental energy in an attempt to prove that wine is cheaper than beer.

Christmas interrupted this somewhat austere regime. Jeremy brought his latest girl-friend home, and two friends of ours came to stay. We felt we had to give one or two parties to entertain them and also to repay debts of hospitality that had mounted up during our lean period. Our staff — all two of them — were of course invited in for a drink and to receive their presents. We had asked Henry, Mrs. Selby's husband, to come as well, and as their son-in-law had provided us with our Christmas tree, which came from a friend of his who was a forester, we asked him and his wife to the party, too, together with Mr. and Mrs. Selby's three grandchildren. This was the beginning of a Christmas party which has become an annual event.

In those days this party was enlivened by Jeremy's *penchant* for practical jokes. For some years he showed great ingenuity in finding novelties. For Alfred's benefit — he is a chain-smoker — there was the exploding cigarette. Among many other tricks there was the fake glass of beer, the glass that groaned when lifted, the buttonhole that squirted water, the cockroach among the mince pies, and the bogus chocolate biscuit. We never dared to use the cushion that made a rude noise when sat on.

Each year we think our Christmas Tree looks more lovely

49

than the last one, and it is always with mingled feelings of regret and relief that I put the decorations away in their boxes for another year — regret that the fun is over and our guests departed, relief that life can settle down into a less hectic pattern, and that I need no longer spend quite so much time in the kitchen. In the New Year the bills come in to confirm that the party is over and that there is work to be done.

It is comparatively easy to work in the winter, when the garden is either frostbound or under snow, and a biting east wind is blowing off the North Sea, making the peafowl huddle behind bushes, sitting on their poor cold feet, with their heads under their wings. Dusk comes early, and it is a relief to be able to draw the curtains and shut out the bleak landscape and the low, grey sky, against which the elms look black and bare. The last chores are done; one can settle down to work to the accompaniment of the soft hiss and murmur of the wood fire — we have never burnt a single lump of coal since we lived at the Manor.

With the appearance of the first snowdrop under the sycamore tree comes a weakening of the determination to work. At odd moments John and I are both seized by an urge to drop everything and go and look at the outside world. Soon there are drifts of snowdrops white as the vanished snow; the aconites growing in the rough grass down the drive lift golden faces to a pale sun; the early crocuses appear under the apple trees and down the Long Walk, and a thrush sings in the orchard. Very soon the garden will be bright with daffodils — we have planted thousands since we came to the Manor, specializing in the early and more delicate species.

It was at this lovely time of year that we decided to go to a sale in North Suffolk. A great eighteenth-century mansion was in process of being demolished. A large part of the sale consisted of acres of paving stones from the gardens, many urns and other ornamental stonework, and hundreds of yards of stone balustrading. Of course we wanted to see the house, and we wanted to buy two stone balls to replace some crumbling ones on a garden wall.

Although this was not one of the houses we had wanted to own — it must have had twenty bedrooms — it was sad to see the demolition in progress. Inside the house doors and fireplaces were being ripped out, and the banisters taken from the wide staircases. Outside, smooth lawns were torn and trampled; there were muddy gaps where there had once been stone steps, and the stone balustrading along the terraces was broken into sections. I felt almost ashamed at being there. Our presence seemed to condone the destruction. However, there was a large crowd of cheerful sale-goers who seemed to suffer no such qualms.

We fought our way into the marquee in good time for Lot 289, only to learn that our stone balls had been withdrawn from the sale. It is, of course, disappointing not to get an item because the price goes too high, but it is even more maddening to be deprived of the chance to pay too much for it. John was very angry indeed. I knew that look on his face, and I moved closer to him. But neither my hoarsely whispered protests nor my fierce nudges could stop him relentlessly topping the bidding for Lot 292 — four stone obelisks, each five foot high.

Now *I* was very angry indeed. 'There goes all the money you got for that article you wrote. And what possible use are they? You just felt you had to buy something!'

'But you don't realize,' protested John, 'all this garden masonry was designed and laid out by Sir Charles Barry.'

'The Bank will be jolly interested to know that, I'm sure,' I said bitterly.

'. . . . . the architect who designed the Houses of Parliament,' John continued, regardless. 'He also . . . . . .'

'Really, you might credit me with a little general knowledge. And *do* stop lecturing,' I said.

It wasn't the time or place for an argument, and John, perhaps wisely, left me raging and went to pay the bill.

When he joined me again there was a satisfied smirk on his face, and he was rubbing his hands together — a characteristic gesture of his when he is pleased or excited. 'I have just sold two of the obelisks to a dealer for what I gave for them,' he said, offhandedly, 'and he is going to deliver the other two to us free of charge.'

'You have missed your vocation,' I said, tartly. But I had to smile in the end.

We put the two bones of contention one each side of the Long Walk, and now that the yew hedges on either side of them have grown up head-high, I have to agree with John that Sir Charles Barry's obelisks make a very elegant feature of our garden.

16 ❀ ARAMINTA and Arabella were making their second attempt at maternity and had been sitting for about two weeks, when one morning I saw, from the landing window, John hurrying towards the house. He usually comes upstairs to enliven my domestic chores with a report on his daily nest inspection, and to tell me of any items of interest observed on his walk round the garden. But that day he went straight into the kitchen where Mrs. Selby was washing up. Mrs. Selby washes up with an impatient energy that produces a bang and clatter reminiscent of hailstones rattling on a tin roof. John had to raise his voice above the din, and I heard him mention Araminta.

I ran downstairs. 'What about Araminta?' I asked.

John was looking rather pale. 'She isn't on her nest,' he said, 'and I can't find her anywhere in the garden.' He put his hand on my shoulder. 'There are a lot of feathers lying round the nest.'

At that time we hadn't become inured to the tragedies that can happen in the peafowl world, and this news was such a shock that I promptly and involuntarily burst into tears. Mrs. Selby looked at me in horror and dropped a cup on the brick floor. 'O dear-o, M'am, you 'ont want to cry,' she said, almost chidingly. I realized that the mistress of the house was expected to keep a stiff upper lip, so I dried my eyes as quickly as possible.

John and I went out to the nest, which was in the hedge by the avenue of cherry trees. The six eggs were unbroken, but the long grass round the nest looked much more flattened than it should have done — a peahen leaves very little trace of her comings and goings. Feathers were scattered all round the nest and over the grass. They were delicately speckled, and were obviously feathers from Araminta's breast. This made me want to cry again.

We started to investigate thoroughly, and saw tracks in the grass as if something had been dragged through it. A few yards

53

farther on, by a depression in the grass, we found a heap of black tail feathers. Then we walked over every yard of our property, but we saw no sign of Araminta herself.

During several previous nights Lucifer had screamed. Peacocks are good watch-dogs when they hear sounds they dislike or are unaccustomed to, and in the face of the evidence we thought it possible that someone might have seized Araminta, dragged her through the grass and put her into a sack where we had found the last bunch of feathers. In view of this suspicion we thought it right to let the police know, and we telephoned our local constable, who came up at once.

P.C. Deben obviously found this assignment an interesting change from hunting escaped Borstal boys and checking gun licences, and he took it very seriously. He examined the eggs carefully, and any minute I expected to see him check them for finger prints. With furrowed brow he paced slowly backwards and forwards round the scene of the crime. His rather heavy tread left the grass considerably more flattened than had the activities of the criminal. We kept Deben refreshed with cups of tea and helped in the search. But the sad and weary day came to an end with no solution of the mystery.

After breakfast next day Deben was with us again. He and John once more started quartering the large paddock. It wasn't very long before John called Deben over. Under a hedge between the paddock and one of the Selby's meadows lay Araminta's body. Her head and neck were missing. The mystery was solved. To bite off the head of a victim is the unfailing sign of a fox.

We have never known whether we had somehow missed Araminta's body the day before, or whether a fox or some other animal had dragged it back through the hedge. We are inclined to the latter theory, as we had searched so thoroughly.

The day before we had sent an advertisement to the local newspaper, offering a reward for news of Araminta, alive or dead. We telephoned to the paper to cancel the advertisement, and a reporter came up to get a news story. I have always felt grateful to that reporter. Dear, gentle Araminta, who must have fought so gallantly to defend her eggs — at least she had a splendid obituary. The newspaper described her as 'a beautiful bird and a wonderful mother.'

17 ✤ ARAMINTA'S disappearance had immediately posed the problem of what to do with her eggs. We had covered them up while we made our initial search for her, but we didn't know how long she had been gone from the nest and we knew we must act quickly if there was to be any chance of hatching them. Arabella couldn't take on any more; in any case Araminta's eggs would hatch before Arabella's, and her reputation as a mother stood very low with us.

When we returned to the house to telephone the police, Mrs. Selby was full of ideas and almost dancing with eagerness. She had that morning put a broody hen in a coop. It was, she said, a fine big hen — a Rhode Island Red — and she proposed that we put the eggs under the hen over at the farm, to avoid disturbing her and wasting time. When, and if, the eggs hatched we could then bring the whole family over to new quarters. This seemed a sensible idea, so Mrs. Selby bustled off to get the hen settled in a sitting-coop, and John followed her over to the farm with the eggs in a basket.

During the next two weeks Mrs. Selby spent more time cherishing that hen than she spent 'at ours', as we say in Suffolk. I think her nights were uneasy, too, because although she says that normally she never dreams, twice she told us that she had dreamt of looking under the hen and seeing a lot of little fluffy chicks. It would be sad for everybody if the eggs didn't hatch, but we were far more worried on Mrs. Selby's account than on our own. Her disappointment would have been intense.

But the day came when Mrs. Selby hurried down the drive almost at a run. Breathlessly she told us that when she had opened the coop that morning there really *had* been some little yellowy-brown heads peering out through the hen's feathers. We all hugged each other with delight.

We brought the hen and the chicks over in the coop, and

56

put it into the big pen which had the shelter attached to it. We had fixed up some perches — known in Suffolk as 'perks' — at varying heights.

The hen and four chicks settled down well. We kept the bars up in front of the coop for two days, but very soon the chicks were running in and out. After that we let the hen and chicks loose in the pen, which was proof against the assaults of any animal or bird. Remembering the disastrous results of keeping chicks permanently in a run we very soon let the whole family roam in and out at will, just shutting them in at night.

Of course there were certain difficulties. That old hen was a devoted mother, but she couldn't at first understand that the chicks expected her to pass them food from her beak. *They* couldn't understand why she didn't do this, and would jump up at her, hopefully pecking at her beak, her comb and her wattles. She didn't enjoy this much and must have been very puzzled, but she was very patient and uncomplaining. She would assiduously scratch up the ground for them, offering them succulent sections of worm, but the chicks in their turn were puzzled about this, and would look uncomprehendingly at the offering.

There was also the bed-time problem. The chicks wanted to start roosting on the lower perch long before the hen considered they were old enough to roost. They would huddle together on the perch while she called to them distractedly from the coop. They would jump down and force their way under her wings, only to sally out again when one bolder than the rest decided to return to the perch.

We never interfered, and left matters to sort themselves out. Eventually that dear old hen became more like a peahen than a domestic hen. She stopped digging up worms for them, and learnt to hold insects in her beak. She would 'point' at flies and moths that had settled on leaves and twigs. She forced herself out of her cosy coop to sit on the perch and spread her wings over four rapidly growing chicks. Before misfortune reduced their numbers her poor wings were extended to their limit. The chicks would jockey for position, nearly knocking her off the perch. She was maddened by their hopping up and down while they got settled, and altogether the bedtime antics of the family reminded us of an act by the Crazy Gang.

Although she had neither the size nor the wing spread of a peahen, that hen was fiercely protective of her charges. She was a heavy bird and she didn't hesitate to hurl her weight at any creature she thought might be threatening them. Cats, ducks and peafowl were all forced to keep their distance, and we humans took care to wear gloves and protect our legs when we wanted to catch a chick.

18 ✤ THE adventures and misadventures of our peafowl
inevitably became a regular topic of conversation
amongst our friends and neighbours. There seems
to be a sort of *mystique* about the peacock which intrigues
almost everyone. John's hairdresser, for instance, whom he
visited once a fortnight for twelve years or so, until the old man
retired, never let a single session in the barber's chair pass without asking for the latest progress report on egg-laying, hatching, moulting, or whatever was going on at the moment.
Walking through the streets in Ipswich John would often be
hailed by some acquaintance with the somewhat equivocal
words, 'How's the bird?'

Two friends who take a special interest in the peafowl, because they themselves are always surrounded by animal life in
one form or another, are Lord and Lady Hawthorne. John was
only fifteen when he first met Toby Hawthorne, and I have
known his wife Felicity for more than twenty years. Indeed, we
first came to know and love Suffolk during visits to their house,
and it was they who took us in while we were waiting for the
workmen to move out of the Manor.

Toby Hawthorne, although he has devoted himself unself-
ishly to public service — politics, the County Council, educa-
tion, hospitals, and so on — all his life, is one of the least conventional men I know. Amongst other things he is an authority
on British mammals and other lesser forms of animal life. One of
the lesser forms was a tape worm which, for a while, Toby used
to carry round in a test tube in his waistcoat pocket. He would
produce this nonchalantly when there was a conversational lull
in any gathering. He would insist that it was biologically most
interesting and everyone must examine it. He would express surprise and disappointment if anyone showed distaste, and listened
to the squeals of the squeamish with a blandly innocent grin.

As well as the cats and the dogs in the Hawthorne household
there was usually some small animal that had been rescued from

disaster in its infancy by one of the children. I well remember the tiny hare, with huge eyes and ears which seemed as large as its body, that the youngest child, Liz, carried around in a large pocket. There was also the red squirrel that survived for quite a long time before Liz overlaid it in bed one night; this nearly broke her heart.

Felicity Hawthorne suffered a good deal in the cause of science, not always gladly. She would sometimes find the oven of her Aga filled with large lumps of clay, which Toby had put there to dry in order that fossils could easily be crumbled out of them. He was highly indignant when she turned them out so that she could cook the dinner.

She never knew quite what she would find in the refrigerator. There was always the chance that a selection of dead mice of different kinds might be packed into the ice-making box until such time as Toby had leisure to dissect them — a job he always liked to do in the drawing-room, usually when there were guests. It was never safe to pick up any stray box that might be lying around the house: if it didn't contain live mice or a ferret it might be full of uncommon spiders.

The Hawthornes have a large family, and their house is usually bursting and bubbling with the children, their friends, and the Hawthorne's own friends and relations. Meals are informal — noisy, rather restless, and eaten at the long table in the big kitchen. One of the most memorable meals, however, which we have had with the Hawthornes was — or started off by being — a rather more formal occasion. They had asked us over to dinner to meet an eminent university professor, who was staying with them after attending the prizegiving at some school nearby.

On this particular evening dinner was to be in the dining-room. We sat over drinks in the drawing room, where the conversation was general, and, presumably out of deference to the guests of honour, Toby did not produce the tape worm.

Nor were we invited to examine the corpses of any animals, large or small. The professor and his wife had been delayed at the school and were rather late, so by the time dinner was announced the after-glow had faded from the sky, and it was very nearly dark. Felicity said she didn't like eating by half-light, so the heavy curtains were pulled across the big windows of the dining room and the six candles in the candelabra on the table were lighted.

Felicity and Toby sat at each end of the long table, almost lost in the shadows. I sat next to the professor. The candle flame was reflected in the polished table and the gleaming silver. The food was delicious, and the whole atmosphere was agreeably civilized.

Toby seldom drinks anything — although he can be more entertaining on tomato juice than most people are on gin — but Felicity's cocktails had been strong and dry, and the wine was excellent. I have a fairly strong head, but when, out of the corner of my eye, I thought I saw a small, dark shadow flash across the wall opposite me, I wondered if I should have had that second Martini.

When, a minute later, I saw that the first shadow had been joined by a second, I decided there must be something wrong with my liver. Really, I wondered, was I becoming a case for Alcoholics Anonymous? I looked round surreptitiously, but everyone seemed to be eating and drinking quite happily, and to be unaware of anything untoward. I decided that, if this was to be the last evening I was going to have a drink, I had better have another glass of wine.

I needed that glass of wine. It wasn't long before there were four shadows wheeling across the wall. I noticed, with the detachment of the doomed, that they were speeding round anti-clockwise. I had read once that one should try and ignore an hallucination, so, although I had lost my appetite, I think I managed to talk coherently and not too feverishly, and I tried not to look at the wall. At least, that is, until I noticed that there was an inner ring of four dark objects going round the room in the same direction, only nearer to the table.

Although I *felt* perfectly all right — if a little confused — I thought perhaps I had better signal John that I felt unwell, and leave the table to people who obviously held their drink better than I did. I was about to try and catch John's eye, when the professor said to me very quietly, 'Do you see what I see?'

I turned to him with such a feeling of relief that I could have hugged him. No longer feeling I was an alcoholic or a psychiatric case, I was able to look the shadows boldly in the face.

'Yes, I hope so,' I said. 'Eight shadows swinging round the room? What on earth are...... ? Oh, my goodness!' I gasped, realization dawning on me with a suddenness that made my heart lurch.

The inner circle had got faces. Little mouse-like faces, furry bodies and leathery wings. The larger shadows the four cast on the walls as they swung round the table became unimportant. I was far too frightened to appreciate the aesthetic or theatrical qualities of the scene — the dim light, the flickering candles and the whirling shadows. As one of the four dived at a candle I dived under the table.

But one cannot remain forever hiding from bats under a table, gazing at the feet of one's fellow guests, while one's host and hostess remain apparently unconcerned, and the conversation flows on normally. So, red in the face, I emerged, and tried to behave as if dining with four bats was a usual occurrence. The professor was a great help, and entertained me with academic anecdotes while pretending, with true courtesy, not to notice every time I ducked.

Towards the end of the meal one of the other, apparently fearless, guests *did* say he thought it unusual to get four bats flying round a dining table simultaneously.

'Oh? Well, I don't know,' said Toby. 'These live up in the curtains all the year round. I'm hoping they will breed.'

19 ❋ ARABELLA'S eggs were not due to hatch for about two weeks after Araminta's. After the first tragedy we had rigged up a protective fence of wire netting around her nest, but at a sufficient distance to enable her to fly off without hitting it. About two days before we reckoned they were due to hatch, John had to be away in London for an evening. I had shut up the hen and her family, and was preparing a hasty supper for Miles and myself before going over to a concert at Aldeburgh — Miles was staying with us for the Festival — when with a terrifying cackling Arabella flew off the nest for the second time that day. She landed near the house and paced wildly backwards and forwards, looking distraught and dishevelled.

I hurried out and gave her some food, thinking how typical it was of Arabella to be so tiresome when we were in a hurry. She didn't appear to want food, neither did she show any sign of going back to her nest. So I heaved a sigh of exasperation, pulled a saucepan off the stove, and went out to see if anything was the matter.

Arabella's nest was at the far end of the longest paddock. When I reached it and saw the sorry sight it presented I really wished that we had never decided to keep peafowl. Of Arabella's four eggs two were lying outside the nest with the shells broken and bloodied, curled up inside were the tiny chicks. They looked as if they were almost ready to hatch. One egg had disappeared entirely; one was still in the nest and seemed unharmed.

Whether Arabella had done this horrid deed herself during one of her periods of diminished responsibility, or whether it was a rat, a weasel or a carrion crow, I shall never know. The evidence of the missing egg rather indicated a rat as being the culprit. But I knew that Arabella would never return to the nest, so I picked up the unharmed egg and ran back to the house. I wrapped it up carefully in a warm towel and put it in a basket

63

at the bottom of the airing cupboard, near the hot tank. I could do no more.

I didn't really want to go off and leave my egg, but neither did I want Miles to miss the concert. We hastily swallowed a drink to calm our nerves, and left for Aldeburgh. We ate cheese, chocolate and apples in the car, and between mouthfuls speculated despairingly on possible causes of the tragedy while twenty-five miles passed under the wheels.

When Miles and I got home, late that evening, the first thing I did was to go to the linen cupboard and look at my egg. Not unnaturally it looked exactly the same, but I imagined that I could hear a very faint sound of tapping. I thought it was probably only wishful thinking, but before going to bed I damped the egg thoroughly, and arranged the warm towel more loosely over it.

Although it is said that hope springs eternal in the human breast, I didn't really believe that egg would hatch. I thought it might well be the one infertile one out of the clutch. So when I opened the linen cupboard door early next morning I found it difficult to believe the evidence of my ears. From the covered basket came the sound of chirruping. It sounded quite a strong chirruping — even a little impatient. When I lifted up the towel there stood a perfect chick, dry and fluffy and quite free of the shell. It was trying to move around in the basket. On only a few other occasions, when I have managed to re-suscitate an apparently dead animal or bird, have I enjoyed such a feeling of reward.

If Miles has a fault as a guest it is that he is rather difficult to rouse in the mornings. But that particular morning I managed to imbue him with some of my delight and excitement, and he was up in good time, gazing rather blearily at the basket in the linen cupboard.

When John has to be away for the night, he always rings me up at nine o'clock the next morning. That morning I waited

Proud Father

Hen and chicks

impatiently for his call, bursting with news both good and bad. He took both kinds calmly, and, perhaps rather sensibly, damped my no doubt premature enthusiasm by saying that he thought it would be very difficult to rear the chick. This pessimistic outlook seemed to me to be so entirely out of character that I assumed he must have a nasty hangover after his night in town.

Because I had called it 'my egg', the end product of that egg became known as Meg, and I devoted the next few days of my life to her. I transferred her from the small basket to our large, well-padded cat basket, in which she had room to move about. I concocted for her delicious dishes of hard-boiled egg, chick meal and finely chopped onion tops. I included some flies I had — with some repugnance — killed on the windows. The first few meals I pushed down her throat with the end of my little finger. But she quickly got the idea, and was soon pecking the food off my finger tip. At intervals I poured a little water down her throat from an egg spoon.

Meg thrived. After several days I realized that she must get proper exercise and, if possible, live the life of a normal pea-chick. The great question was whether the foster hen and also the other chicks would accept her, and whether Meg, having adopted me, would take to them. I thought I had better not disturb the family by trying to put her under the hen at night, and I decided to infiltrate her casually among them at feeding time. I gave the hen and the four chicks a good portion of food, and while they were busy with it I carried Meg out and put her down amongst them.

It was a hazardous moment. I hated throwing Meg out into the harsh world. She looked so much smaller than the other chicks, and so bewildered. My feelings were a little like those I had suffered when seeing Jeremy off to his first boarding school. But I needn't have wasted so much emotion. Meg soon started pecking at the food, and I heaved a sigh of relief when I saw that the other chicks took very little notice of her. The old hen stopped eating, looked at Meg and just bunted her once with her beak. After that she seemed to accept her as one of the family.

The whole happening has always seemed to me something of a miracle.

The fact that Meg was smaller than the other chicks, and not so strong on her legs, made it difficult for her to keep up with them. She would get left hopelessly behind. I spent a good deal of time during the next few days retrieving Meg from her last stopping-place and carrying her over to her companions. She seemed pleased to get these 'lifts' and as soon as she was put down would scurry to join the other chicks. Then there was another problem. Whenever Meg saw me anywhere in the garden she would leave the other chicks and rush to meet me. This, of course, meant that she was again separated from the family, and had to be carried back.

I suppose, in the light of subsequent events, the whole operation could be regarded as a waste of time. But I think there are few happenings in life that can be written off as a complete waste — although I suppose that depends on what one expects from life. I only know that I have seldom felt as satisfied and well rewarded as I did during the days I 'wasted' over rearing Meg. Nor have I ever again had so close a relationship with a bird.

Except for Meg, who remained rather small, the chicks soon grew as big as their foster-mother. All went well until they became infested with red-mite. We should, of course, have dusted the hen with some anti-pest powder, but we had been in such a hurry to get the chicks under her that this had been neglected. The vet prescribed for us a nicotine preparation which we were to paint on the perch. The chemist who sold it to us said it was the right strength, and told us how much to paint on the perch. Alas, he was wrong on both counts. When

John went to let them out of the pen next morning he saw a sad sight. Three of the chicks lay dead, evidently poisoned by nicotine fumes. The poor little things had managed to get off the perch and had struggled out into the pen. There they had died, and Meg was among them. Well out of Mrs. Selby's sight, I shed a few bitter tears.

The remaining two chicks did well. They and their foster mother were inseparable, and they made a comical trio. It wasn't until early the following year that the dear old hen felt her duty was done. One morning John was working in a room in the attic. Hearing a noise on the landing, he opened the door. There, having negotiated two flights of stairs, stood the hen and the two large chicks.

The hen seemed restless, and John decided to take her back to Mrs. Selby. Five minutes after Mrs. Selby restored her to the flock she laid an egg on the ground. She had been unable to wait to get to a nest box. Seldom have I heard of a greater devotion to duty.

Her former charges went round for two days croaking miserably, and returned to the pen at night. But at last they decided to stand — or roost — on their own feet, and chose a bedroom in the communal oak tree.

20 ✿ SOON after the two surviving chicks were left
        on their own, we realized that they were a cock
        and a hen. John has a cousin living in Worcester-
shire, and as we had promised to sell her a pair, if and when we
had one available, we thought she had better have Cocky and
Girly. We had called them by those rather silly names as it
didn't seem worth the trouble of thinking of better ones when
Jan might want to re-christen them.

Jan and a friend came up from Worcestershire for the night,
and most of the evening was spent in instructing her in the
ways of peafowl. She was enchanted with Cocky and Girly,
and set off next morning in an agony of apprehension lest they
should suffer any discomfort on the journey. They arrived in
Worcestershire safely, but apparently found it difficult to settle
down. For some weeks the telephone wires grew red hot — and
the telephone bills mounted — with frantic appeals for help and
advice from Jan, and our return calls when we thought of some
fact that might be useful to her. But eventually the birds
settled down. Jan never gave them other names, and, as far as I
know, they are Cocky and Girly to this day.

About midsummer we decided we must get another breeding hen to replace Araminta, and as company for Arabella, who
seemed lost and lonely without her sister.

The new peahen arrived in July, and after a period in the pen
she was duly let out to make the acquaintance of her new husband and his wife. She disregarded Arabella, but she adored
Lucifer, and from the first moment she pursued him with
passion and determination.

We couldn't have chosen a worse moment to present him
with a new wife. Having just lost his long train, and also his
voice, Lucifer was feeling thoroughly inferior and unsure of
himself. He didn't want any truck with a member of the
female sex, and he would lurk behind the yew hedges, just
glancing through gaps and peering round corners when

68

something aroused his curiosity. But the new hen would always track him down.

A desperate chase would ensue. Lucifer, without the burden of his tail, would run like a racehorse, his blue neck outstretched and his long legs flashing. The hen could not run quite as fast, but she would follow relentlessly — we could almost imagine her gritting her beak in her determination to get her man.

This marathon continued daily for some time, the hen pursuing the object of her passion with untiring zest. Lucifer now lived in a state of abject terror of his new wife, and we only saw him when he was running. One day he scrambled through a hole in the hedge and raced down the road. Nothing daunted, the hen followed him, although we made a vain effort to stop her. An hour later Lucifer came home, alone.

Although we searched, made enquiries everywhere, and also advertised, no one seems to have seen that hen again. What is even more curious is that she was never heard, because peahens cannot help cackling loudly when they fly down from a tree in the morning. Naturally we minded the financial loss, but we had had no time to grow fond of her or even to give her a name. So we were not heart-broken.

Lucifer, for his part, was mightily relieved.

21 ❧ THE time had passed so quickly and pleasantly since our last financial crisis, with much of interest going on in the house and garden, and among the livestock, that we had rather put finance out of our minds for the time being. Our plans for Retrenchment through Austerity and Hard Work had probably not been put into operation for long enough to be effective, so I suppose we should not have been surprised and shocked when we heard the Wolf — disguised as our Bank Manager — at our door once more. There was no time to reproach ourselves for being a couple of weak characters who were not very good at arithmetic. Some quick action was needed.

John sold to a bookseller friend a large part of his collection of eighteenth-century poetry — first editions which he had lovingly accumulated over the years. But that was not enough. With heavy hearts we did the only other possible thing. We rang up the agent who had been our liaison with Miss Boult and asked him how much he could get us for the Manor, and whether he had any other cheaper houses on his books which might suit us. We didn't even stipulate that it must be suitable for peafowl.

His answer to the second question was 'Not at present.' His answer to the first made us think there must be a Guardian Angel who looks after improvident fools like ourselves. He told us that Miss Boult had arrived back in England the week before, and had already been asking him about the Manor. In view of the fact that we had bought a small piece of extra land from the Selby's, and had made a few minor improvements in the house and a great many in the garden, he thought it likely that Miss Boult, who desperately wanted the Manor, might make us a bigger offer than her previous one.

Miss Boult did make us a bigger offer — a substantial offer. Her only condition — a quite reasonable one in view of our previous shilly-shallying — was that we would let her have our answer within a specific time.

Sad and chastened, we started house-hunting again. Even though our standards were considerably lower than before, for a time the prospects seemed hopeless. But our quite undeserved good luck held. We heard, through a friend, that a house where she had once taken us visiting was coming into the market. It was about seven miles from the Manor, and we hurried there at once.

On our previous visit to this house our preoccupation had been social and not architectural, though we did remember the beautifully moulded Jacobean plaster ceiling in the large bedroom. Now that we looked at the house with the eyes of prospective purchasers we realized that in time — after we had made some alterations, of course — it might be a house in which we could bear to live. Even more important was the fact that the garden was eminently suitable for peafowl.

It was an Elizabethan house, built of stud and plaster, and colour-washed the orangey-red so familiar in Suffolk. It even had a block of four octagonal chimneys. These had been cemented over, presumably to save the cost of repair, but we knew this was a small defect that could easily be put right. Of course the interior needed some alteration to make it perfect, but we felt that with Miss Boult's good offer we could afford to do this. At this time the house had home-made electricity, and although the garden had endless possibilities — it was moated on three sides and contained some fine tall trees for the peafowl — it needed a great deal doing to it. There were some derelict barns that would have to come down. But because of these liabilities the owner was asking a relatively low price, which we thought we could afford.

The owner was courteous, sympathetic and considerate. He was anxious that we should have the house, and he allowed us to go over it whenever we wanted and roam around at will, while we planned alterations that experience should have taught us would undoubtedly consume the margin of capital we needed to put us on our financial feet again.

To some extent this planning — and the fact that we had found a house that wouldn't separate us from the peafowl — helped to make bearable our sadness and chagrin at having to leave the Manor and all we had done there. This time we had taken Mrs. Selby into our confidence at the beginning, and she understood the whole situation.

So involved were we with all these arrangements that — although I am a little ashamed to confess it — the invasion of Suez and the subsequent political crisis did not mean a great deal to us at the time. When we rang up the agent to give him our acceptance of Miss Boult's offer — well within the time limit — we were surprised to learn that she had considered it advisable, in view of the international situation, to return to the United States for a time.

This was extremely awkward. The man from whom we were going to buy the house was waiting for our firm offer. We couldn't make it until we knew definitely that Miss Boult was going to honour her offer to us.

The agent had the address of her solicitor, but not her own. The agent cabled our acceptance of Miss Boult's offer; we also cabled our acceptance. Nothing happened. We waited impatiently, and then cabled again.

Meanwhile the owner of our new prospective home was also, not unnaturally, waiting with some impatience. We could not expect him to wait forever. The day came when he rang up to say that he had received an offer which, in the absence of a firm one from us, he felt he must accept. We entirely understood, but after our visions, so nearly realized, of having both an interesting house *and* some money in the bank, we felt more miserable and uncertain than ever before.

However, we didn't have to suffer the uncertainty for long. By the second post that same day we received a letter from Miss Boult's solicitor. Although it dealt us a financial blow, we found, to our surprise, that it also brought us a tremendous sense of relief.

We danced round Mrs. Selby in the kitchen crying, 'Hurrah for Nasser!'

She must have thought we were mad. But the solicitor's letter was both an enormous relief to us, and extremely funny. He explained that he could not advise Miss Boult to go ahead with the purchase of the Manor as, owing to the Suez crisis, it seemed possible that she would not be able to obtain enough oil fuel for the central-heating plant she had intended to instal. He ended with the words 'If the international situation should turn in favour of Miss Boult, I will communicate with you again.'

Apparently it never has.

22 ❋ IT has always seemed odd to me that the two brief appearances of Miss Boult in our lives have not, in fact, changed anything. These two episodes were so overwhelming at the time, and seemed fraught with significance. During those periods we felt that the pattern of our life was going to be changed. If I were writing fiction, it would have been changed. But, looking back, it just seems that much energy and emotion was wasted to no good purpose — as though someone had started to write a play and had torn it up before it was finished.

It is true that these crises kept our feet on the ground and our noses to the grindstone, and that out of them John produced some of his best work. They proved, too, that we possessed the not altogether admirable British characteristic of being able to muddle through. But hard work, austerity and muddling through were not enough to give us the wherewithal to repair our crumbling Tudor ruin, which was in urgent need of attention.

As the Manor was scheduled as a building of Historic and Architectural Importance, we felt that the Authorities ought to help us with its upkeep. We had read a good deal in the newspapers about grants being made to the owners of crumbling houses like ours for necessary repairs. We therefore applied to the appropriate body for a grant for necessary repairs to the Manor. In due course a day was arranged for Experts to visit us, inspect the house and discuss an estimate with a builder. Out of consideration for everyone's purse, and with memories of the Factory Act and all the electrical appliances, we did not choose *the* Builder this time, but found another small local firm.

The Experts were due to arrive at eleven o'clock in the morning. As it seemed probable that they would still be with us at one o'clock, we had asked them to stay to lunch.

Should we give them bread and cheese and cider for lunch, so that they fully realized our poverty? Or should we give them a reasonably good lunch, accompanied by some wine, in the hope that it would make them feel friendly and sympathetic? I thought that a meal consisting entirely of bread and cheese might give them indigestion, which would certainly prejudice our chances of getting a grant. So I decided on a chicken casserole, with home-grown vegetables, a simple sweet, and then cheese. John thought that we might have a bottle of modest Alsatian wine with the lunch without appearing too rich to require a grant.

The Experts arrived promptly at eleven o'clock. Apparently they had spent a most uncomfortable night at an hotel, after inspecting someone else's picturesque ruin. They sank into deck-chairs on our lawn with sighs of relief, and gratefully accepted the mid-morning coffee we offered them.

They did not seem to be in any hurry to look at the house, and we sat in the sun, lazily chatting, and rather avoiding the issue.

Eventually the builder arrived and they reluctantly got up out of their chairs and set off to do some inspecting. I was busy in the kitchen and did not go round the house with them, but, as John told me afterwards, it was obvious that the chief Expert's real enthusiasm was for Georgian and Victorian architecture, and that Tudor and Elizabethan houses interested him not at all. When John remarked that one day he hoped to convert our hideous Victorian annexe into something more shapely and in keeping with the rest of the house, our Expert sprang hotly to its defence.

When the inspection was over and the builder had departed — no doubt hoping that a remunerative job was in the bag — the Experts flopped back into their deck-chairs again, first pulling them back into the shade. After a hurried consultation in the kitchen we decided that it might be good policy to offer them a drink, as they were manifestly exhausted. Also, by that time we rather wanted one ourselves.

They accepted the offer gratefully, and expressed a preference for gin. As lunch was more or less ready, I joined the group under the trees, and very pleasant it was to sit down. John was giving them a lecture on the history of the Manor, which they listened to with charming courtesy as they sipped their gin. We offered them another drink.

Those Experts certainly enjoyed their work. As the level of the gin in the decanter sank, their spirits rose. Any slight awkwardness inherent in the situation disappeared. The conversation became gay, lighthearted and inconsequential. We were all friends together. Indeed, we discovered that one of the Experts was a second cousin of a great friend of ours. And the other was an enthusiastic book collector. At that point John disappeared into the house, and put a decent Moselle into the refrigerator instead of the Alsatian wine.

When the gin decanter was empty we went into lunch. Lunch was a success. The chicken turned out to be delicious and the wine was even better. We discovered more mutual friends, and John opened a second bottle. The conversational level may not have been as high as I felt it was at the time, but the talk flowed merrily and easily. The object of this operation was temporarily forgotten. The inspection had become a party.

When the last mouthful was eaten and the wine bottles were empty, we adjourned to the garden with coffee and brandy. It soon became obvious that the Experts were not going to do any more inspecting. They lay back comfortably in their deck chairs, sipping their brandy and smoking cigars. This, one felt, was the sensible, civilized way to deal with affairs of Historic and Architectural Importance to the community.

The somnolent calm of the afternoon was suddenly broken by one of Lucifer's more strident shrieks. The Experts jerked themselves awake, looked at their watches, and exclaimed in horror. They said they should have left two hours before. Even then it took them some time to prise themselves out of their chairs. We all weaved our way round the house to their car, a vintage Bentley, the bumper of which was being fiercely assaulted by Lucifer.

Everyone shook hands with everyone else. The Experts kept saying 'thank you' for hospitality received and how lovely it was after the hardships they had endured in other places.

We thanked them warmly for coming. Plans were made for future meetings. At last, with everyone waving and shouting goodbye, the old Bentley shot off down the drive, swerving from side to side, hotly pursued by Lucifer.

John and I congratulated each other on a successful day, and went indoors to sleep it off.

No grant was ever forthcoming.

23 ❖

THE peafowl are not the only birds that live with us and depend on us for their comforts.

One of the first things we did in the garden, during the first dry summer, was to clear out what remained of the moat that originally surrounded the house, remove all the rubbish, bottles, broken bricks, bicycle tyres, and old bedsteads that had accumulated over the years, and renew the land drains that fed the moat. Before the moat had even refilled the first wild duck — ancestress of many generations of mallard that have since bred here — flew in to look the property over.

Evidently word got around that the water was sufficiently nourishing, and, what was more important, an abundance of food lay about in the garden waiting to be picked up. There must have been a rumour, too, that the human beings seemed friendly and considerate. Very soon after the arrival of the duck, a drake flew in, followed by more ducks. Since that time the mallard population has increased annually, and I have often seen as many as twenty-five waiting impatiently outside the kitchen door for their evening meal.

They literally sing for their supper, if their raucous 'quack' can be called singing. Mallard are very intelligent. They have a habit of glancing at us sideways out of one eye, and that bright, beady eye misses nothing that is going on. At the slightest movement in the kitchen, or if they hear any significant noise such as the larder door opening, they are instantly on the alert and shouting hoarsely.

Sometimes, especially in the breeding season, the clamour mallard make can be almost as nerve-racking as the outraged, piercing shrieks that Lucifer utters when a jet aircraft hurtles overhead. It is the ducks, of course, who make all the noise; the drakes can only quack very softly.

A few years ago we had a duck living here who persistently woke us up in the small hours by walking round and round the house vociferously protesting that she hadn't eaten for twenty-four hours. As she passed noisily under the bedroom window I would wake up with a start. I would doze off as she disappeared round the corner of the house, only to be jerked awake again as she reappeared a few minutes later. There were moments when I not only longed to wring her neck, but very nearly got out of bed to do it.

Across the road from our front gates there is a long, wide stretch of moat, part of a complicated moat system that surrounded this whole property before it was divided up, and before the road ran as it does now. The mallard like a change and spend quite a lot of time over there. There is a constant traffic backwards and forwards between the two moats. They prefer to fly when they have no young, and the splash of several mallard landing on our moat, and the beating of wings when they leave us for other waters, are sounds we love to hear.

When there are ducklings, everyone has to walk. The ducklings follow their mother in a solemn, sedate procession — usually strung out in a single line — down the drive, under the gates and over the road to the big moat. This trek is later repeated in reverse. Alas, some never get across the road alive. Private motorists and motor cyclists are their worst hazard. The lorry drivers are usually very careful and considerate, tiresome though it must often be to have to slow to a standstill while a duck and as many as fifteen duckings waddle across the road.

For many years now ducks have nested in the garden. Some of them chose discreet and well-hidden places such as ditches and hedges, but others have, I suppose, become tame enough not to worry, and we find nests recklessly exposed to view in flower borders, under rose bushes, and in the short grass round the edge of the moat.

Several years ago two ducks nested cheek-by-jowl on the bank. In fact the two nests looked as one, and eggs overflowed from one to the other. The ducks often changed ends and sat on each other's eggs. The day came when most of one clutch hatched off, and in due course the ducklings were marched into the water, whether by their real mother or not I do not know. At this point the other duck evidently decided that it must be *her* eggs that had hatched; she had sat long enough and her patience was exhausted. So she got up and joined her nest-fellow in the water. We thought at first that she was just taking her rest period, but she didn't return to the nest.

It seemed a sad waste, since the abandoned eggs must have been so nearly ready to hatch. But we realized that, even had we had time to bother and could have found one, a broody hen was not the answer to this problem. Ducklings need to take to the water soon after they are hatched.

However, we had not reckoned with the power of the midday sun. When we went into the garden before lunch, the sound of eggs chipping in the nest could be heard quite a long way off. We were appalled at the thought of all those orphans coming unsheltered into the world. We felt we must do something. So we started a desperate salvage operation. In a nearby nest sat a duck whose eggs were almost due to hatch. Wearing gloves to protect our hands from her furious pecking, we put under her several of the eggs that had only just started to chip. But there was a limit to the number she could accommodate. So, as the rest of the ducklings chipped their way out, we helped the tiny, wet, floppy little objects out of the shell and put them one by one into a basket in the linen cupboard to dry off.

Late that evening, when they were dry and feeling much stronger, we infiltrated the ducklings under two ducks — one in the neighbouring nest who had now hatched off but had not yet left the nest, and another that was brooding a very young and newly-hatched family under the willow tree.

It wasn't possible to assess accurately the success or otherwise of this exercise in interfering with nature, because the mortality rate among mallard ducklings is always very high. Ducks are fierce and devoted mothers, but do not seem able to control

. . . . *the mallard population increases*

The moat in winter

their ducklings or to keep them together. Like the Old Woman who lived in a Shoe, they have far too many children, and as they cannot count, they often fail to notice that one or two of their brood have failed to negotiate a high grass edge to a path, and are lying on their backs, yellow bellies uppermost and legs kicking in the air, wildly struggling to get on their feet again. If one of us is not about to put them right side up and restore them to their negligent mother, they die of exhaustion. Also their daily walk backwards and forwards across the road takes its toll, and of course any stragglers become prey to cats, rats and predatory birds.

Undoubtedly our efforts did save a good many ducklings. The two foster-mothers went about with very large broods, and, after they had made their initial protests of hissing and pecking at us, they did not seem to resent the interlopers. The question of whether or not the effort was worth while does not really matter. We knew that we had — and still have — too many mallard roaming round our garden, but the urge to try and save a life — even that of a tiny duckling — seems irresistible. I hope it isn't merely a kind of human vanity. I don't think it is.

Our moat is also a favourite nesting place for moorhens. A moorhen will rear several broods in one season, but they never seem to hatch more than five or six chicks. These are fascinating little creatures, and at first look like a small ball of coal-black wool. At this age they are shy, and lurk under the banks of the moat most of the time. However, I think our moorhens become more tame than is usual — we have seen them boldly taking food from under the beaks of mallard and peafowl — and when the chicks are a little bigger they begin to come ashore. At this stage they are still black, but their legs have grown long and lanky and their feet huge. They always remind us of Ronald Searle's black-stockinged school girls from St. Trinians.

After the 'St. Trinians' stage the young moorhens develop into elegant, graceful birds, with soft, grey plumage and long grey legs. We call them 'teenagers'. By the end of the summer they are wearing their adult dress of black, and above their green stockings they wear a red 'garter'. Their movements are jerky — they jerk their red-billed heads when swimming, and when nervous they jerk their tail, with its white under-side.

It is widely believed that moorhens are dangerous companions for other water fowl and will deliberately drown ducklings. This has caused some prejudice against them. We have been observing their habits for a good many years, and have never seen any moorhen even threatening a duckling. If there is any drowning to be done, the mallard are more likely to be the ones to do it. They are bad-tempered birds, and will peck viciously at each other's ducklings whenever they have an opportunity.

Moorhens have some very endearing qualities, one of which is a strong family feeling, shared by every member of the family from the parent birds down to the smallest chick of the latest brood.

We have often watched with interest the parent moorhens foraging in the paddock for food. When they have found a dainty morsel they run and give it to the nearest 'teenager' who may be on the lawn. This one gives it to another 'teenager' who passes it to a 'St. Trinian' near the moat. The 'St. Trinian' then takes the food into the water and feeds it to one of the tiny black chicks. The chicks will be fed in this charming manner many times in the day. We have never seen the slightest display of animosity between any of the different age groups of moorhen, and I won't hear a word said against them.

24 ✤ IN the Spring of the year that was memorable for the enjoyable but unrewarding visit of the architectural experts we had bought a new pea-hen, Matilda, as company for Arabella. This time we had chosen a more sensible season of the year in which to present Lucifer with a new wife, and, although she did not breed that year, Matilda settled down well. She is still with us, a calm, sensible bird and a good mother.

A strange thing happened. With the advent of Matilda, Arabella's attitude to maternity underwent a change. We had always allowed her to sit, in the hope that she would rear her chicks, as it is less complicated than giving them to a broody hen. We merely put the eggs or the chicks under a hen when Arabella was overtaken by one of the disasters she positively seemed to attract.

This year, however, Arabella laid five eggs, and sat for twenty-eight days without anything untoward happening. On the day when she was due to hatch we were, as usual, apprehensively alert, and kept our eyes turned in the direction of her nest. We were prepared to rush and fetch a broody hen from Mrs. Selby the moment we saw that Arabella had resentfully blossomed into motherhood.

Towards the end of an anxious day the moment arrived. We saw Arabella advancing down the Long Walk. To our astonishment, not only did she appear to be quite calm and collected, but she seemed 'whully proud.' She obviously had no thought of pecking at the four chicks that clustered round her, but she was lifting her feet high and carefully, to avoid stepping on them. When the little party arrived on the lawn, Arabella immediately sat down and brooded her chicks. We kept a sharp eye on her for several days, but we needn't have worried. Arabella had turned over a new leaf; she was now an exemplary mother.

Arabella brooded her chicks on the ground at night for a few days, until they could manage to run up the sloping trunk of an old apple tree in the orchard, and roost on a low bough. When they were about four weeks old she decided that they could quite well leave the nursery and move to the oak tree bedrooms. This move was a little premature, but such over-optimism was not peculiar to Arabella. Our peahens always try to take their chicks up the oak tree before they are old enough. The hen flies up, and, instead of waiting on the lowest bough, she proceeds, branch by branch, until she is almost at the top of the tree. There she sits, clucking encouragement to the puzzled and anxious chicks on the ground far below.

Usually on the first two or three nights of this attempt to get the chicks up the tree the hen eventually realizes that the situation is hopeless. She flies down, and hurries them off to the safety of the apple tree. By the fourth or fifth night mother is adamant. The children really must make an effort.

By this time John has put a step-ladder on the lawn under the oak tree, and has placed a plank with one end on the steps and one on a low wall, in such a position that a chick who manages to get on the plank should be able to fly onto the lowest branch. From there it has to make its own way upwards to its mother.

The first night of the new regime is hazardous, and one of us has to be at hand in case of emergency. There always *is* a state of emergency. Chicks vary considerably, both in the strength of their flight and in their intelligence. Some will fly onto the plank and from there to the first branch without much difficulty. Some fly onto the plank or the steps but do not understand what they have to do next. Just when we think that they have got the idea, down they fly again, all of a twitter.

It is unfortunate that the tree is against a wall that divides us from our neighbour's stackyard. The real trouble begins when, panic-stricken — it is getting dark and they have nowhere to go — one or two chicks flutter onto the wall and get under some wire netting on the wrong side. This means that one of us has to go round to the yard and try to chivvy them back again. If they stay on the wall or get tangled with the wire this can be managed. But if one or more flies down into the yard, runs under some farm implement, or perches on the guttering of a barn, it sometimes seems a hopeless task to round them up, especially if one is single-handed. One has to try not to fluster the chicks — and to keep calm oneself — and edge them into some corner, or against the wall, where they cannot take to their wings. With luck they can then be picked up and put back over the wall. Sometimes all goes well after that, and they find their way up the tree. Sometimes the whole caper starts all over again.

On several occasions, when there has been a particularly small or weak chick, John has had to put the long ladder up against the tree, carry the chick up to its mother, and put it under her wing.

We were especially thankful when Arabella's four chicks learnt to climb to bed unaided, without meeting with any of the usual disasters that seemed to dog Arabella's families. We enjoyed standing under the tree in the dusk, looking up into the mass of green leaves and twining branches, and listening to the chirruping and chattering of Arabella's chicks as they made their way up the tree, jostled for position under her wings, changed places and changed again, and eventually settled down. Soon we could hear nothing but the leaves rustling in a soft breeze.

Although we only had the one family, that was a happy breeding season. Arabella's chicks all survived, and it gave us great satisfaction to see her pride and contentment. She was, that year, one of the best mothers we have ever had. She had also managed to plan her family well — two cocks and two hens. This suited us. We had a friend who wanted to buy a cock, another who wanted a pair, and we had already decided to keep one hen for ourselves. That hen, Priscilla, is with us today. Like her mother, she is given to high-flying and hysteria. She is a better mother than was Arabella at her worst, but not so good as was Arabella transformed.

After we had parted with three of her children in the New Year, Arabella seemed to pine, although Priscilla was a devoted daughter, and rarely left her mother. We noticed that Arabella walked rather slowly, and was not so eager for her digestive biscuits. Her coronet seemed to droop a little, and her eyes looked faded and dull.

Of course we had never known how old she was when we originally saved her life and brought her to live with us. We were worried by these signs of advancing years. As a precaution, we gave her an anti-biotic capsule, and I made her tempting dishes of hard boiled egg and chopped cheese. She still managed to get up the oak tree to roost, and we hoped she would pick up when the warmer weather came.

One morning Arabella and Priscilla were not waiting in their usual places by the kitchen door. From across the orchard came the sad cry a peahen makes when frightened, distressed or lost. We ran across the orchard and saw Priscilla pacing up and down outside the peafowl pen, uttering her mournful cries. We didn't see Arabella until we went into the pen and looked in the little shed. She had crept quietly in there, laid herself down on the straw, and died.

Dear Arabella, if in her life she had sometimes seemed a little wild and unbalanced, in her dying she was truly dignified and, I hope, at peace.

25 ⚜ PRISCILLA was too young to breed in the Spring following her mother's death, but in the next year we had one of our most successful seasons. Matilda and Priscilla each hatched four chicks. By the time the first frosts were whitening the grass in the early mornings, leaves off the elm trees blowing into golden drifts over lawns and drive, and smoke from bonfires hanging like mist over the empty fields, they were each walking four large, healthy children round the garden.

Apart from daffodil time, when our garden glows with every shade of yellow and gold, I like late Autumn, with its crisp, almost intoxicating air, and the colours — from gold to deep red — burning in woods and hedges, as much as any other time of year. Indeed it seems to me to have a less obvious and far more subtle charm than Spring.

This should have been a particularly enjoyable Autumn. We had weathered the year financially and were still happily here. We were looking forward to Christmas more than usual, as Jeremy and Maureen were bringing our grandson down for his first Christmas at the Manor — indeed, his first Christmas anywhere. The peachicks had been safely reared, and good homes were waiting for all of them.

But Fate, perhaps in order that we should not suffer *hubris*, placed a small fly in the ointment of our content. This was the nagging anxiety that teased our minds whenever we read in the local newspaper that Fowl Pest had been detected somewhere in our part of the world. At first this worry was almost unconscious, and we didn't talk about it much. The outbreaks we read about were fairly far away, and, in any case, the few people we knew who also kept exotic birds agreed that peafowl were immune to Fowl Pest.

As the year drew towards its end Fowl Pest gradually grew nearer to us, until at last we were encircled by a ring of infected farms. Everyone now had solemn stories to tell of whole flocks of poultry being slaughtered overnight.

It was said that birds were merely stunned by a blow from a stick, and were then buried alive. Any goose or duck that was foolish enough to show its bill round a corner was set upon and killed at once. At one farm, so the story went, the slaughterers entered the farmhouse and, deaf to the entreaties of the farmer's wife, took the pet budgerigar from its cage and strangled it.

Our fear was no longer subconscious; we were forced to face it. What worried us was the fact that in some cases poultry kept anywhere near an infected flock were arbitrarily slaughtered without the humane preliminary of a blood-test. Of course we hoped desperately that the Pest would be checked before it got any nearer. But we felt uneasy all the time, and we tried to arrange our lives so that there was always one of us at home in case the worst happened — the worst, of course, being outbreaks of Fowl Pest on one or other of the farms on either side of us. The general attitude was that any birds living anywhere in the vicinity of an outbreak of the disease were potential carriers of it and must therefore be eliminated.

The reports of the callousness of the slaughterers had raised my Irish blood to boiling point, and I was prepared to defend Lucifer, Matilda, Priscilla and the chicks with the .22 rifle if necessary. John, who is more peaceable by nature, quite rightly disagreed with my attitude, and did his best to calm me down and cheer me up. Although we could hardly bear to speak of it, we did agree that, if the worst happened, we would have no dealings with official slaughterers. A close friend and neighbour, who is a crack shot, promised to deal with the matter.

Preparations for Christmas kept me fully occupied, but every day brought, instead of a growing feeling of pleasurable anticipation, an increasing uneasiness. When we came home

88

from a morning's shopping, we could never be certain that bad news would not await us.

The blow fell two days before Christmas. Mrs. Selby hurried round earlier than usual in the morning to tell us that several of the Selbys' hens were dead and many more seemed ailing. Henry was certain it was Fowl Pest.

The Government at that time did not pay compensation for birds that had already died; so, to save themselves from loss, and for obvious reasons connected with the slaughterers, Henry and his brother Cecil had decided to do their own slaughtering at once, and not wait for the overworked Inspector to take a blood test. Mrs. Selby, who was near to tears, mainly I think on our behalf, had come to warn us to expect a visit from the Inspector as soon as the Selbys' outbreak had been reported.

That period of waiting for the Inspector to arrive was as nerve-racking an experience as we have ever gone through. Even the postman's step made me feel as if my heart had stopped for a moment. And it was such a long wait. But for the sake of everybody we made a determined effort, during Christmas Eve and Christmas Day, to forget the threat that hung over our family of birds. Little Heywood was too young to realize that perhaps our Christmas Party was less gay than usual — he simply lay and laughed at the baubles on the Christmas Tree. We all did our best, and having Jeremy and Maureen with us — they were not, after all, so involved — was a great help.

So another Christmas passed, if not quite as usual. I think to an outsider it would have appeared to be a merry one. We had all been asked out to lunch on Boxing Day, and we persuaded Jeremy and Maureen to go, while we stayed at home and looked after Heywood.

I gave Heywood his lunch early, and put him in his cot to sleep. We were just settling down by the fire to have a drink in the first peace and quiet we had known for four days, when the front door bell rang.

It was an unlikely hour for any of our friends to drop in, and I think we both knew who it was. 'It had to come, you know, darling,' John said.

It was perhaps rather mean, but I suddenly remembered I had a saucepan on the stove. 'You go,' I said. I went in the direction of the kitchen, leaving doors open, and tried to hear what was going on at the front door, although I didn't really want to. I heard John say, 'Good morning' in a rather unnaturally bright voice. All I could hear of the visitor was a low rumble.

'Yes, this is the Manor,' said John. And then more rumblings.

'No, we have no poultry at all,' said John. Another rumble.

'Well, yes, we do keep some peafowl, but surely they are known to be immune?'

I do not know who had told the Inspector that we had peafowl. It would not have been the Selbys, who were as worried about them as we were. 'Dew anything happen to that lovely bird I 'ont be able to face you,' Mrs. Selby had said. I suppose it was just that there are no secrets in the country.

'Do come in for a minute,' I heard John say, after some further conversation. 'It may take a little time to get them together.'

As my heart sank, my blood pressure rose. I decided that my place was by John's side in the fight, so I joined them in the library. I meant to be charming but I fear that I was bristling.

I saw a rather small, middle-aged man, looking tired and harrassed. And then I nearly laughed outright, in spite of myself, because he carried, rather gingerly, a syringe nearly as large as a bicycle pump.

'Mr. Smith wants to take a blood test of the peafowl,' John said.

'I would have been here earlier,' said Mr. Smith, ' but I've been out all through Christmas. Never known anything like it.

I have to go on to a farm at Framlingham, so I mustn't be long now, if you don't mind,' and he sank into an armchair.

The situation was not nearly so bad as it might have been, and John and I gave each other a reassuring glance. I felt the time had come for me to exercise a little charm. 'You must be absolutely exhausted,' I said sympathetically.

'Well, I won't deny it's been tiring.'

'You've time for a quick drink, surely?' said John. 'You must have earned it.'

'Well, I mustn't stay long,' repeated the Inspector. 'A small sherry, perhaps?'

John fetched him a large sherry. Mr. Smith looked a little less tired by the time he had finished it. As there was no point in avoiding it, we eventually got onto the subject of Fowl Pest.

'Of course,' said Mr. Smith, as he drank his second sherry, 'Chickens are always dying of something. In some cases they haven't died of Fowl Pest at all, and the farmer knows it. But the compensation is often greater than the value of the flock, and he prefers the money. If it wasn't for the compensation we should hear less about the Pest, and I shouldn't have to be out all over Christmas.'

'I must say,' said John, 'it's extremely hard on *you*.'

'Of course,' said Mr. Smith, as he drank his third sherry, 'I don't know if your neighbour's birds had Fowl Pest or not. They are all dead and buried now. It sounds as if they might have had it; that's why I must test your peacocks. Things being as they are, we can't afford to take any chances,' he added, trying to sound official.

'Our birds hardly ever wander out of the garden,' I said meekly.

'I suppose they are in a pen?' said Mr. Smith.

'Oh, no,' said John, as he handed the Inspector his fourth glass of sherry. 'They walk about wherever they like on our property. We have eleven at present.'

To say that Mr. Smith looked startled is an understatement. He took a gulp of sherry and nearly choked. 'Eleven!' he said, putting down his glass with a shaking hand. 'When you said you had to get them together I thought you meant a pair of them, and I didn't realize they wouldn't be in pens. We really must get started,' he added, with a worried frown.

'Some of them are quite small,' said John, comfortingly.

Mr. Smith drained his glass, and heaved himself reluctantly out of his chair. 'How do you suggest we catch them?' he asked.

'I haven't really worked it out,' said John. 'Perhaps we could drive them into one of the pens, but it may take some time. You'll have to be careful that the peahens don't go for you,' he added. 'They are fierce and protective mothers.'

'Don't forget this,' I said, handing Mr. Smith his gigantic syringe.

'I should think we had better start with Lucifer,' said John, leading the way out of the porch door. 'He may be the easiest to get into the pen. I had better warn you though that he hasn't been caught or handled since he came here, and he isn't going to like it.'

We found Lucifer lying in a patch of weak winter sunshine in the moat garden. As we approached him he got to his feet, re-arranged his six feet of glittering train, and looked at us haughtily.

'Come along, old boy,' said John. 'Come along to your pen for a biscuit.' But I noticed that John hadn't got a biscuit, and also that there wasn't a long, thin stick at hand. In these circumstances Lucifer had no intention of going anywhere; he merely moved closer to the brick wall.

Mr. Smith looked unhappy. 'I had forgotten they are so big,' he said. 'I've never had anything to do with peacocks before.'

I was beginning to feel quite sorry for Mr. Smith, but I

couldn't help rather enjoying the scene. 'Perhaps you could catch him in the angle of the wall,' I suggested.

'Well, if I can, would you help me hold him?' the Vet said to John, nervously.

'I don't want to seem unco-operative,' said John, 'but I don't want those spurs of his to tear this particular pair of trousers. Yours look fairly thick.'

'Perhaps you could take him by surprise,' I said.

'But do be careful,' John said. 'I wouldn't like to guarantee that it will be his blood that flows,' he added, with some relish.

Poor Mr. Smith turned red, and then it seemed that *his* blood drained from his face. He took a step towards Lucifer, his freedom of movement rather impeded by the syringe. Lucifer, offended by this over-familiar approach by a stranger, carrying a strange-looking weapon, refused to budge an inch. He drew himself up to his full height, and fixed Mr. Smith with a basilisk stare, his bright brown eyes glittering.

I don't know whether he was motivated by desperation or by a false courage out of the sherry bottle, but Mr. Smith took another step forward. Lucifer drew back, turned his body sideways, put his head down, and looked up at the Inspector out of one eye.

We knew of old what these actions portended.

'Look out!' cried John, 'he's going to jump at you.'

Mr. Smith stepped back hurriedly and dropped his syringe. But, having wound himself up for the attack, Lucifer couldn't stop. He jumped into the air, his legs, with their sharp spurs, extended in front of him, and his wings out-stretched. Mr. Smith having moved back, there was, luckily, nobody in the way. His impetus carried Lucifer to the edge of the moat, so that he was forced to take to his wings. He flew across the water and didn't stop flying until he was up on the roof of the house.

The Inspector picked up the syringe, and looked at his watch. 'Oh, goodness,' he said, 'I should have been at Framlingham hours ago. I think, you know,' he added, not looking either of us in the face, 'we shall have to take the word of the bird experts that peafowl are immune to Fowl Pest.'

As Mr. Smith drove off in his car, Lucifer, from his perch on the roof, gave a threefold shriek that we very rarely hear in the winter months — the shout of triumph over a vanquished and retreating foe.

26 ✤ WHEN John had a novel published in 1959 we naturally hoped it would be a success, but we never dreamed it would sell as well as it did. When, a little later, he sold an option on the film rights, we were jubilant. Although the sum of money involved was comparatively small, with our usual improvidence we started to discuss plans for the further restoration of the Manor even before the money was safely in the bank.

It had been obvious for some time that something would have to be done about the ugly Victorian annexe that formed an East wing to the house. John had been using one of the bleak, damp little rooms in this wing as a study. When the ceiling of this fell down onto his desk, and part of the mouldering floor gave way, his working conditions became just too uncomfortable. We realized we should either have to pull the annexe down, or rebuild it.

We had established sometime earlier that this annexe was built on Tudor foundations. In fact the first five or six courses in the walls were of thin Tudor bricks. In the sixteenth century it was not unusual for the kitchen to be in a separate building which would stand a little apart from the house. We think that this was almost certainly the case here, as there seems no evidence of an original kitchen anywhere inside the main building. This decided us to reconstruct the annexe using the existing walls, rather than to pull it down altogether.

Had that been his chosen profession John would have made a good architect; he is also a very useful bricklayer. He soon produced plans — both of the interior and of the elevation — for turning the annexe into the very pleasant Georgian-style building it is today. Not only does it comprise a large Garden Room, but he also managed to fit in a cloakroom, boot-room and wine cupboard as well.

We knew from bitter experience the cost of employing a

95

firm of builders, and we were lucky to find Herbert to work for us. Herbert is a bricklayer and general builders' labourer by trade. He had left a firm to become a freelance, and at that moment was out of a job and badly needed work. John had to be in London two days a week, but he thought he could give enough time to supervising Herbert, helping him with any job that needed two people, and 'scheming things out' — a passive and often lengthy operation much favoured by every craftsman we have ever employed in Suffolk.

Herbert is a hard worker, and it didn't take long to reduce the annexe to its basic four walls. While this purely manual work was going on John was not idle. Down in the valley an ancient workhouse was being demolished — Dickens is supposed to have used it as his model for the workhouse in *Oliver Twist* where Oliver 'asked for more'. From the demolition contractor we managed to buy five genuine mid-Georgian sash windows, complete with frames and the original glass panes, at a cost of £1 each. If we had had them specially made I suppose they would have cost at least £25 each.

Over the matter of flooring, too, our luck held. We heard that a part of the old barracks at Colchester was being pulled down, and from there we bought, very cheaply, enough good maple wood boards for our Garden Room floor. It is true that here and there on them you can see the marks where the rapacious and licentious soldiery stubbed out their cigarettes; but hard work with a sanding machine has removed most of them. From another demolition we added sufficient old flat tiles to our existing hoard to assure us of a good roof.

With only one bricklayer, an occasional day's work by a plumber, a few hours' help from a visiting carpenter who came to put the floor down, and supervision by an amateur foreman who could only attend to his duties between bouts of authorship, the conversion took a fairly long time. Getting the roof

The new Garden Room, with Sir Charles Barry's obelisks in the foreground

Herbert at work

on was a particularly tricky job for two people. I didn't feel at all easy until it was finished and I saw Herbert and John safely back on the ground, with no bones broken.

During the reconstruction several interesting fragments of sixteenth century architecture turned up. On the side of the annexe by the little courtyard we found a flight of old steps. It was, however, impossible to see from whence they came or where they were leading to without digging up more of the garden than seemed sensible. We also discovered an old well, quite close to the steps. This had been largely filled up with ancient bricks, presumably taken from the Tudor building that stood on the site. Among the bricks were several pieces of pottery, dating from medieval times to the eighteenth century. For some years we have collected old pottery, and it was interesting to see that some of the fragments we dug up were almost identical in material and design with some seventeenth century 'blue-dash' chargers which we have hanging on the walls, or the eighteenth century brown slipware dishes that stand on the old oak tables in the hall.

We also dug up the bones of a great many animals — at least we hope they had been animals. Sometimes we feel that it would be both interesting and informative to open up all the old moat system, and excavate the whole garden. But, alas, life has become too short.

I think Herbert was sometimes lonely when working on his own, so he would sing to keep himself cheerful. He has a long, rather lugubrious face and rarely smiles, and there was a certain incongruity in his hoarse and decidedly un-tuneful voice rendering his versions of old favourites such as 'No, no, Nanette', 'These Foolish Things' and 'If you knew Susie'. After going through his repertoire two or three times he would switch to hymns.

Suddenly, in the middle of a hymn, a recalcitrant brick would irritate Herbert beyond endurance. Out would flow a stream of four-letter words, addressed to the brick, which he would slap furiously with his trowel. Having chastized it sufficiently, he would fetch another brick and happily resume his recital of 'Tea for Two' or 'Onward Christian Soldiers'.

27 ❀ MANY people believe that peacocks are vain
creatures. Indeed, it is difficult to imagine that
so beautiful a bird in his full glory could be
anything but vain and pleased with himself. The peacock's
natural walk — with or without his full plumage — is a rather
exaggerated strut. There is also the fact that a peacock will
look at his reflection — in a window, a shiny car bumper or
wheel hub, a looking-glass or anything at all that will reflect
his image — for hours on end.

Having studied Lucifer for eleven years I realize that he does
share some characteristics with the average human male. He
is proud, rather touchy, and very obstinate. He can be gentle
and affectionate to his women-folk. On the whole he is bold
and brave; but I have seen him put on a somewhat cowardly
and undignified exhibition when one of his hens was faced
with an unexpected threat to her eggs. He makes a great show
of running about at top speed and shrieking, but that is all the
help he gives.

He is determined to teach his children to keep their place,
especially his sons, even if he has literally to jump on them.
These admonitory lessons usually take place at meal times, and
I fear they are often prompted by greed. But I do not think
that vanity in the accepted sense, which seems to me to be an
essentially self-conscious emotion, has any place in his make-up.

I am sure that the explanation of Lucifer's preoccupation with
his reflection is a simple one. He thinks he sees a rival peacock,
threatening his territory and his women. That his attitude
towards this 'rival' is so much more belligerent during the
mating months would seem to me to prove the point. When
he has lost his train, and is feeling inferior, he will still sometimes look at his reflection, but only with the mildest interest.
When he is at the height of his sexual powers, but not actually
displaying, he will stand for hours in front of the glass panels in
the garden-room door, eventually pecking at them fiercely. If

we open the door he will pursue the supposed enemy into the room. We sometimes have to draw the curtain over the window, as he once splintered his beak during a particularly violent onslaught.

We have to keep the gates onto the road shut during daylight hours, before the peafowl have gone to roost, because stray dogs are apt to wander in and frighten the birds. And the peafowl might wander out into the path of farm lorries. This is a nuisance for us when we are coming and going by car, and very tiresome for our visitors, though they are usually very tolerant. But a far more difficult social problem is posed by Lucifer's attitude to any clean, well-kept car that may be parked in front of the house. After he has spent some time chasing his 'rival' from polished wheel-hub to polished bumper, he may catch a glimpse of 'him' in a door. Tantalized and furious at the other bird's elusiveness, he may eventually hurl himself at the door. This treatment does not do the door any good.

Lucifer has a special conditioned animosity towards black cars, because we used to have a black car. It was always coming and going, but was never left standing long enough for Lucifer to catch more than a very brief glimpse of the rival peacock. Lucifer hated this car.

John had a theory that if he were left long enough with it he would get tired of chasing the imaginary interloper and would give up trying. I did not agree but was willing to try anything if it would make this aspect of our life a little easier. Alas, it did not work. I winced each time I heard the bang that meant an attack on the door, but what put an end to the experiment was the sight of the blood streaming from Lucifer's legs where he had cut them on the bumpers. Luckily the cuts were only superficial. But it was obvious that the longer Lucifer was left with his enemy the more incensed he was going to get.

We now have a grey car, and Lucifer is not nearly so interested in this. The reflection is nothing like so clear. Possibly, too, he is growing older and more staid. But we still do not dare to have visiting cars parked in the drive in the day time. For weekend guests there is room in the garage. If we have a handful of friends in for a drink they have to leave their cars in the road, and walk up the drive. If we have a large party Lucifer has to be enticed into his pen with the aid of digestive biscuits or a large looking-glass, and left there until the guests depart.

A year or two ago we had an evening party in September, and it was necessary to park cars all the way up the drive. It was almost as though Lucifer knew what was afoot. He stubbornly refused to be inveigled into his pen on any pretext whatsoever. We had to give up. We comforted ourselves with the thought that it would be almost dusk before the first car arrived, and with any luck Lucifer would be hurrying off to roost. In any case, we thought, if he did happen to be still around, he would be so confused by the number of cars that he would take no notice. So we left it at that and prepared for the party without further worry.

It was an unfortunate decision. The party went with a swing, and as hosts we were kept fully occupied. I heard Lucifer shriek once, and was fairly certain the sound came from the oak tree. On my way to the kitchen to fetch some hot sausages I caught a glimpse of Alfred — who was helping to park the cars — hurrying about in the gloaming and looking rather anxious, and I assumed that the guests were not parking their cars according to his instructions; they very rarely do.

When the last guest had gone, and Alfred came in for a glass of beer, he looked shattered. He told us that Lucifer had declined to roost, and he had not been in the least confused by the number of cars. He had made his way unhesitatingly to a large black car, charged twice at a gleaming door, and then perched on the bonnet, scoring it deeply with his claws. It was the largest car in the drive; it was a brand new Bentley. This was its first outing since its owner had taken delivery. What I had heard was Lucifer's shriek as he stood in triumph on top of (as he thought) his rival.

The Bentley's owner never told us about the incident. The sad story was confirmed by some friends who arrived late. When we asked the owner of the car about the damage he admitted rather wryly that here and there on the car were some rather deep scratches. But although we implored him to do so, he resolutely refused to send us the bill. I hope he will have his reward in Heaven.

28 ✤ LUCIFER has one or two curious habits which I have not yet met among other musters of pea-fowl, although of course they may exist. He has one particular foible. This is his refusal to sleep in the same tree as his wives when they are ready to start laying.

He seems to know at once when they are in this interesting condition, and from that moment nothing will induce him to roost in the usual oak tree in the front of the house. He now goes to bed in a large oak tree in the smaller paddock at the back of the house. This is rather tiresome of him because, should he be noisy at night, the Selbys hear him more clearly. He sleeps there until all the eggs are laid, and the hens are sitting properly, when he will return to the communal oak tree in the front. Once he is re-settled there he doesn't seem in the least worried by all the clucking, croaking, flying up and down and other antics which, in their early days, attend the chicks' bed-time.

Lucifer has an odd taste that I feel must be unusual in a pea-cock — he loves milk. We discovered this by chance one day when we were having tea in the garden and put down a saucer of milk for one of the cats. She turned up her nose at it — probably it wasn't sufficiently creamy — but Lucifer arrived on the scene, dipped his beak in the saucer, thought about it for a moment, and then continued drinking it with relish.

Perhaps 'drink' is not quite the right word. He doesn't drink it in the same way as he drinks water — taking a mouthful and tipping his head back, as all birds do. He takes a mouthful of milk and seems to chew it. Then he swallows it as he would something solid. But, whatever his method, the milk disappears quite quickly.

There are occasions in the lives of Lucifer and his wives and children when all go on a party together — I think 'orgy' would be a better description. These orgies take place during the late summer, when the winged ants are hatching out in great numbers — in the grass and in the brickwork of garden walls and the walls of the house. The whole peafowl family becomes what Mrs. Selby describes as 'crazed' over these. Having discovered and eaten one lot of ants they all hurry round the garden in pursuit of more. The more they eat the crazier they get, and the more eagerly they rush around to find the next hatch-out. In short, they appear to become hopelessly drunk on the formic acid that is in the ants.

During this annual beano Matilda and Priscilla abandon all responsibility for the children, who are scattered all over the garden getting noisily tipsy on their own. By dusk the whole family presents a disgraceful sight. Their necks are stretched out, their wings are drooping nearly to the ground, all their feathers are ruffled and their coronets are awry. They are all extremely bad-tempered, and the quiet of the evening is broken by screams, honks and the continual hoarse croaking they keep up as they avidly pursue their tipple.

By evening they are forced to walk with extreme care, lifting their feet very high. Lucifer looks especially funny because he has such long legs. He walks with the exaggerated and impossible dignity — except when his feet don't go down where he expected — that can only come out of a bottle.

Bedtime is bedlam. None of the birds can fly straight, and the chicks have to make several attempts before they land on the right branch. They are all much more vocal than usual. The hens — themselves feeling very precariously perched — are clucking furious instructions to the chicks, and the chicks are croaking in alcoholic despair. Although it is too late in the year for him to be in full voice, Lucifer adds to the noise and confusion by trying to produce one of his more piercing shrieks, an effort which nearly topples him off his branch. Altogether the goings-on must equal any scene from *The Drunkard* or *Ten Nights in a Bar Room*.

29 ❧ ALTHOUGH we have long realized that the older one gets the more quickly the years pass, it did seem to us that the tiny, sardine-like fish given to us by Toby Hawthorne, when we first opened up the moat, grew into sizeable carp in an astonishingly short time. Of course it must have been much longer, but it didn't seem much more than a year later, when Alfred came to us one evening, almost speechless with excitement. He gestured in the direction of the moat, so we went with him. When he was able to speak he told us he had seen six fish swimming just below the surface of the calm water, in the shadow under the big willow tree.

It took our eyes a little time to get accustomed to looking into the water — occasionally a small breeze would ruffle it, and we would have to start again — but very soon we saw them for ourselves. It was the first time we had seen them since we had put them in, and we were nearly as excited as Alfred. Although it was difficult to guess accurately, they looked about nine inches long.

From that day on they seemed to increase rapidly in size, weight and numbers. In the following years we began to see different generations of fish, ranging from five or six pounders down to hundreds of small fry. Had they all survived the moat would have been solid with fish. For many months of the year they were invisible, buried deep down in the mud. We would usually notice them first, as Alfred had done, gliding through the darkening water on a still Spring evening at dusk. When June came, bringing some calm, hot days, we would see the big fish basking near the surface in the shade of the willow tree. They would lie with their big mouths nearly out of the water, opening and shutting them rhythmically.

Neither John nor I are keen fishermen, and although the carp were handsome fish, reddish-gold in colour and beautifully marked, I cannot explain the fascination they had for us. We would stand and admire them for five minutes at a time, as they swam silently under the bank, or basked among the bull-rushes. Then one of us would move and cast a shadow on the water, and with a flick of a tail they were gone.

We thought they would be gone forever during the hot, dry summer of 1959. As the water in the moat sank lower and lower, the bigger fish became stranded on the mud. We spent a lot of time pushing them back into water that wasn't really deep enough for them, and sometimes they received an injury during this operation. There was a large mallard population living with us during the drought — why, I do not know, as our moat at that time could not have been a very satisfying piece of water for them. There were too many fish, and there was no depth of water. Perhaps their presence on the surface irritated the mallard, who attacked them ferociously. They must have killed hundreds of the smaller fish. One or two pecks were enough to kill, but I did see some of the mallard actually eating the fish with apparent relish. There was nothing we could do about this, and we could only look on, frustrated and helpless, and pray for rain.

In the end, as the drought continued, and more and more of the big fish became hopelessly stranded, we decided we must do something. So we removed some of the biggest in a landing net, and put them into a big portable water tank — the sort that runs on wheels. We put some wire netting over the top to prevent them from jumping out. We kept about a dozen large fish alive in this way, until the rain came and broke the dry spell, and the moat filled up sufficiently for us to put them back.

In spite of drought and the mallard it never seemed, later, that there was any lack of fish in the moat, and I think that probably quite a large number of the smaller ones did manage to survive by burrowing into the mud.

We have some close friends in London who come down for a weekend every summer. We flatter ourselves that Edward and Deirdre are fond of us. They also love our house and garden, our cats and our birds and a weekend in Suffolk. But for Edward it was the carp, above all, which made his weekends. If we were enthusiastic about our fish, Edward was crazy about them. His delight in our small piece of water was touching. When breakfast was ready he had to be summoned more than once from beside the moat, where he had been sitting, fish-watching, since the small hours.

Although he is a keen and experienced fisherman, I think Edward's pleasure was as much aesthetic as sporting. He would spend almost as much time watching the water as he did fishing it. Eventually he would get out his rod and start fishing. Deirdre and I would sit in deck chairs, watching him with slightly pitying amusement, and chatting in low voices lest we disturbed the fish.

When Edward caught a fish, it was immediately put into a bucket of water. When the bucket was suitably full, it was John's job to carry it down the drive and tip the fish into the big moat across the road.

Edward caught a great many fish, usually about one pound in weight. Although I know little about the subject I understand they gave him some quite good sport. He was always afraid of catching one of the six-pounders and damaging it. One day he did hook one of these. I can see the expression on his keen, aquiline features to this day — conflicting emotions of horror and excitement. This fish gave Edward every chance of exercising his skill. Luckily for his peace of mind, after a long struggle and some tense moments the fish got clean off the hook, apparently unhurt. Deirdre and I smiled at each other when we saw the look of relief on his face as he sank exhausted into a deck chair.

It usually happened, when the time came for them to leave on Sunday evening, with Deirdre already sitting in the car, that Edward would not be there. But it was not difficult to find him. He would be standing on the lawn by the moat, gazing wistfully at the water and muttering a silent farewell. This always moved us very much.

Edward and Deirdre still visit us but not, alas, to fish. During the bitter winter of 1962/63 the moat was covered with ice for weeks on end. When the thaw came we were away, visiting friends. By the time we got home the ice had gone from the moat. On our usual tour of inspection it was the first place we looked at. The wind was blowing from the south, and the north end of it was solid with the bodies of carp. John removed over fifty from the water, most of them over six pounds in weight. We hoped that some might have survived down in the mud, but Edward, who hopefully fished here last year, said that he was sure there were no fish there.

Some friends of ours, who live in an old Tudor house miles from anywhere, have, in the kindness of their hearts, laboriously caught some small carp in their own moat, and transported them up here in a bucket in the back of their car and put them into our moat. We haven't yet seen any manifestation that we could swear was definitely caused by a fish, but we are hoping that one day Edward will be able to bring his fishing-rod again.

30 ❀ A RECENT and very handsome addition to the bird population at the Manor is Goosey, a Canada goose who flew in during bitterly cold weather two years ago. She had a blue ring round one leg, she seemed tame and didn't hesitate to come for food, but exhaustive enquiries round the neighbourhood failed to find her owner. She settled down as if she had lived here all her life.

Although by nature a heavy, rather clumsy bird, with her buff-coloured chest, her black neck and her white cheeks Goosey looks quite spectacular when feeding among the brown mallard and the grey peahens. Sartorially, Lucifer is her only rival. It must be admitted, however, that her walk is not graceful. She waddles slowly and heavily on enormous black feet that look like a frogman's flippers.

Goosey doesn't like the peafowl, but she has a wholesome respect for them and keeps her distance. When one of them advances belligerently upon her during feeding time it is ludicrous to see that big, heavy body give a frantic leap into the air as she takes avoiding action. But Goosey takes it out on the mallard. With her neck stretched out straight, hissing breathily and rather adenoidally, she will advance on one that has annoyed her, pick it up by the feathers on its back, and toss it over her shoulder. Luckily the mallard are very tough.

Male and female Canada geese are virtually indistinguishable in appearance, and we called this creature Goosey for want of a better name and any information about her sex. During this last Spring our guess was proved correct. Her continual angry scolding of the ducks became more and more continuous, and rather tiresome. Her envious fury when she saw a broody duck was pathetic, but we hesitated to get her a mate in case she was a gander.

One night we were kept awake into the small hours by her usual cries of frustration. We awoke next morning to an unwonted silence. John, glancing sleepily out of the landing window on his way to the bathroom, stopped in his tracks and rubbed his eyes. There on the lawn stood a pair of Gooseys — our own, quietly and complacently preening her feathers, and, beside her, a handsome Canada gander.

We were overjoyed; and so, no doubt, was Goosey. Here was the answer to her noisy prayers. The gander, who wasn't ringed, was not nearly as tame as Goosey. Before he would eat the food we put out for him we had to move well away. Now that we saw them together we could see that the gander was a little larger than the goose, and thicker in the leg.

That day there were no noisy cries from Goosey, and she never once plunged hissing at an inoffensive duck. She and the gander passed a placid and contented day, and we went to bed hoping for a peaceful night.

Alas, we were wakened at six the next morning by Goosey's usual high-pitched bark. When we looked out she was walking restlessly about the lawn, alone. The gander had flown away.

However, poor Goosey's twenty-four hours of love bore fruit. Within two days she laid an egg in an abandoned duck's nest under a rose bush by the moat. Perhaps she intended this choice of a nest to indicate a sort of thumbing-her-beak gesture to the ducks. The prospect of maternity, however, did not calm her irritable nature. When she wasn't sitting on her makeshift nest, she was lumbering after the ducks in a fury, and hissing at any cat that dared to show itself.

Poor Goosey, she must have been hatched under an unlucky star. Someone stole her eggs, one by one, almost as soon as she laid them. In the end she gave up the unequal struggle. Soured, I suppose, by these unfortunate experiences, she made friends with a pair of fine white Aylesbury ducks who live on the moat across the road, and now she spends more time over there than she does here. But I have no doubt that she will be back permanently when the first nip of cold weather gives her an appetite, and next Spring we shall get her a fine gander for husband — with pinioned wings.

31 ❈ SIR LAWRENCE and Lady Grampion, who live at the Old Rectory, are near neighbours of ours as the crow flies but not, alas, by the road which winds, twists, turns and changes its direction several times before it eventually arrives at their gates.

Sir Lawrence has spent a lifetime in the Diplomatic Service, mostly in the Middle East. Life in a hot climate seems to have suited him. He looks half his age; his hair is barely touched with grey, his face looks youthful and unlined, he bubbles with energy and enthusiasm, and has a diplomat's courtesy. When he has kissed my hand with exquisite grace, in a greeting or a farewell, I, too, feel half my age for at least the next ten minutes.

Lawrence has an observant eye, an excellent memory and a keen sense of humour. He is an excellent *raconteur*, and has a seemingly endless store of amusing and sometimes charmingly risqué anecdotes which he tells about life in the Diplomatic Service. Occasionally, I fancy, some of our more homespun Suffolk neighbours find his sophistication a little beyond their grasp. A recollection I particularly cherish is of Lawrence at a cocktail party, giving an erudite dissertation on the sexual significance of leather to a spinster of uncertain age. She was obviously deeply impressed, but totally uncomprehending.

Long before we came to live in Suffolk, and long before Sara and Lawrence joined us here, peafowl were kept at the Old Rectory and used to roost in the huge cedar trees. Perhaps because of this and because his life in the East has made him familiar with them, Lawrence is keenly interested in peafowl. He is a mine of information about oriental history and mythology, and much of the knowledge we have picked up about peacock myths we owe to him.

It is believed that peafowl originated in the Indian jungle and were taken from there to Persia. From Persia they found their way to Greece. Here they were held to be sacred, and to be the favourite bird of the goddess Hera. It is recorded that in

Athens in 450 B.C. they were exhibited at the full moon, which was Hera's day. This veneration, however, does not seem to have prevented those in authority from charging a fee to see the sight, or from selling the eggs.

Indeed, their history is one of contrasts and contradictions. They have been worshipped as angels and as devils — and among some primitive tribes in the East they still are. During his campaign in India, about 325 B.C., Alexander the Great is supposed to have seen peacocks for the first time, glowing like jewels in the jungles. He found them so beautiful that he gave orders that they should not be killed. But they were eaten with pagan enjoyment by the Romans, who are believed to have been the first people to eat them. Two thousand years ago the breeding of peafowl for the table was a profitable occupation in some parts of Italy.

It is probable that the Romans introduced peafowl into Europe. In early Christian mythology the peacock symbolized immortality, and the bird often appears in medieval paintings of the Adoration of the Magi. Much later its status changed again and it appears, not in religious paintings, but in peacock pie, a delicacy much favoured by our Elizabethan forebears at Christmas time. Its gastronomical role only ended when it was superseded by the turkey.

Apart from Burmese peafowl — a larger, darker breed, rarely seen in Europe — there are three distinct varieties. These are the ordinary Indian or 'check-shouldered'; the 'black-shouldered', sometimes called the Japanese peacock, although it has no connection at all with Japan; and the pure white peacock. These last are strikingly beautiful in a rather ghostly sort of way, especially when seen against a dark yew hedge. But they need fine dry weather to show off their charms — in wet, muddy weather they can look very dirty and bedraggled.

Our Lucifer is of the ordinary Indian variety. His wife Matilda would, from her appearance, seem to be of the same

Feeding time

White chick

breed, but somewhere among her forebears a black-shouldered bird has married into the family. We know this because the chicks of the black-shouldered peafowl are almost pure white when hatched, and Matilda's daughter, Priscilla, usually produces at least two white chicks in every clutch of eggs. They become pied as they grow older, and in due course the cock becomes dark and black-shouldered; but the hen always remains lighter in colour than the Indian hen. We have always sold our white chicks, as when they are of mixed parentage they do not breed true, and to us the Indian breed is more beautiful than the black-shouldered.

Again and again, of course, we come up against the ancient superstition that there is something 'unlucky' about the peacock — or, at any rate, its feathers. This superstition is especially prevalent amongst actors. Sir Compton Mackenzie, who comes of a theatrical family, has a quite unreasoning aversion from them. John was once walking through the Royal Pavilion at Brighton with an actor when they noticed a peacock-feather *motif* in the wallpaper; the actor immediately closed his eyes and hurried past with bowed head.

The point of origin of this superstition is presumably the Greek legend of Argus, 'the all-seeing', who had a hundred eyes. The goddess Hera appointed him guardian of the heifer into which Io, a girl friend of Zeus, had been metamorphosed. Hermes, on the instructions of the lustful Zeus, sent the hapless Argus to sleep by playing sweetly to him on his flute, and then cut off his head. Hera, incensed at this treatment of her faithful watchdog, transplanted the hundred eyes of Argus into the tail of her favourite bird.

I fail to see how this makes the eyes in the peacock's tail 'unlucky'. Indeed there is a curious correspondence between the implications of this myth and the early Christian belief that peacocks' eye feathers symbolize immortality. That, at any rate, is the theory I prefer.

32 ❧ ALTHOUGH we have employed some not altogether disinterested persuasion — it would be nice to think of our chicks in that lovely setting — the Grampions decline to resume the peafowl tradition at the Old Rectory. They are afraid they might find the noise too tiresome, the cedar trees being rather close to the house. Perhaps in the Far East peacocks screech all the year round, but here — as we have tried to explain to Sara and Lawrence — they are only noisy during the mating season, and the duration of this is short in a cold, wet year.

Matilda and Priscilla are not capable of making a really disturbing noise. They will 'honk' when they are alarmed, agitated, or merely hysterical. They will utter a continuous, hoarse croak when some mischance or oversight separates them temporarily from their children, or if anything disturbs them during the night. But I must admit that to the sensitive ear Lucifer can be something of a problem. Unless the weather is unseasonably cold we usually begin to hear his more piercing shriek about the second week in April. This comes intermittently during the first few weeks, but works up to a crescendo by the end of May. In June we hear a little less of it, and by the third week he is gradually beginning to lose his voice. Instead of his scream of anger he seems only able to produce a sad, wailing, rather nostalgic cry. He makes this particular cry when any strange car, or lorry, that may have been up to the house, disappears out of our gates, and he thinks he has driven it off.

I sometimes wonder if peacocks were not a good deal quieter before the advent of the internal combustion engine. Of course, Lucifer shrieks when he is displaying to his women folk, and sometimes for sheer *joie de vivre*. But his noisiest demonstrations occur when jet aircraft are roaring overhead, when large, strange, noisy lorries or cattle vans drive into the stackyard near his oak tree, or when any particularly noisy car or motor bicycle passes down our lane. At all these he will rage stridently if impotently. When he has gone up to roost at night it is always a plane or a car that starts him screaming, although, oddly enough, he never shrieks at our own car should we happen to come home late.

Ear-shattering though his screams are if one happens to be close to him, it is a noise one can get used to in the daytime. Indeed, I think we should miss it now, just as we should miss the raucous quack of the mallard. But at night it *can* be disturbing. Partly on our own account, but mostly out of consideration for our neighbours at the two farms, we shut Lucifer into his pen at night during his noisiest period. The pen is much further from the road than his tree, so that he cannot hear any passing traffic, and for some reason, when he is roosting on a perch which is not very far off the ground he seems much less eager to use his voice.

As I have mentioned before, it is not always easy to get him into his pen. A looking-glass or some digestive biscuits may work for a week or two, but then he begins to get suspicious. Sometimes he will deliberately go up to roost very early, and nothing will tempt him down. Or he will allow himself to be lured to within a yard or two of the pen. There he will stop and casually nibble at some grass. Then he will suddenly turn, hop over a low hedge, and run briskly back towards the house.

If we fail to get Lucifer into the pen at the first attempt we know from bitter experience that it is useless to try again. We have to put up with him for that night, and hope our neighbours will be tolerant if he is noisy. They *are* both tolerant and understanding, and I know they bear in mind the nights when a noise like a fog-horn has disturbed us all — the baffled roar of a cow that has lost her calf. There has to be a lot of give and take in country life.

33 ❧ I SUPPOSE all animals, whether furred or feathered, living with people who love them, develop their own marked personalities and idiosyncrasies. Each of our five cats has a completely different character, but they are all affectionate and responsive to a marked degree, and often seem to be more like intelligent dogs, without losing any of their essential 'cattiness'.

They all love a walk. Though there may not be a cat in sight when we come out of the house, as soon as John and I begin to stroll round the garden on a summer's evening we find we are suddenly accompanied by the five of them.

We can no longer accurately work out their relationships, but Teedie, black and long-haired, was our first cat, and is the ancestress of them all. She is seventeen now, and walks very slowly. She stops continually so that we may 'coze' her — a nice Suffolk word meaning 'stroke'. This rather slows up the walk.

Pussin is the youngest, a black cat with a whiter-than-white shirt front and stockings. He is called Pussin as an abbreviation of Puss-in-Boots. He and Toppy, a tortoiseshell, rush to sharpen their claws usually, alas, on the trunk of a young apple tree rather than the stake which supports it. They then go mad, rushing so high up trees that we fear they will never get down. Sometimes they share our apprehensions and sit swaying precariously on some slender branch, calling pitifully for help. If we take no notice they always get safely down in the end.

Tabitha, our tabby — or Cyprus as they are called in Suffolk — will sometimes forget her animosity towards her son, Pussin, and join in the game. But she spits if she finds herself anywhere near him. This is really rather sad, as he is such a friendly cat, and so anxious to please. Captain Scott, our big, lumbering marmalade cat, is, for all his size and his name, very shy and nervous. We usually hear him wailing behind a hedge, feeling he has been left out, but when we call him he will come and join the party. He has occasional moods of gaiety, but spends so much time looking over his shoulder and preparing to run from some imaginary danger that he hasn't much time for fun.

Some sixth sense tells old Teedie when we are going away for a visit or a holiday. For days beforehand she will be perpetually under my feet, and when I am packing she will try to sit in my suitcase. When we come home the same sense informs the cats that it is *our* car, and no other, that is coming down the drive, and usually the five of them will be assembled on the grass circle near the front door to greet us. This welcome makes homecoming especially enjoyable.

Our old house *ought* to be haunted. It is old enough, and romantic enough, and has lots of dark corners. But it is in fact a benign and friendly house, and only one ghost has ever appeared to us. This is so insubstantial as hardly to merit even the description of 'ghost'; but of its appearances we have no doubt whatsoever. Our 'ghost' is a small dark shadow, moving about low on the ground, that both John and I occasionally see out of the corner of our eyes. When we swing round to look at it more closely it has gone.

Sometimes when we have glimpsed it we feel certain that it is one of our cats that must have slipped through the room. But when we investigate we usually find that none of them is in the house. We call this appearance the 'Little Man'. But personally I am sure it is a little cat. Sometimes we both see the Little Man fairly frequently for several weeks at a time, and then perhaps we don't see him for months.

Mouser used to see him far more often than we did. Mouser was a black cat, with slanting yellow eyes. She was a social misfit, and we used to call her the Witch's Cat. We never felt she really liked us, and she hated all the other cats. We would talk to her, 'coze' her, and give her the cream off the milk; but it never made any difference. She would sit, glowering, in a corner by the boiler in the kitchen, and would spit and swear at humans and cats alike when she felt in a black mood.

Mouser was not a playful cat, even as a kitten, because she never liked any humans or any other cats well enough to play with them. But she loved the Little Man (or Little Cat) and she would play with *him* for minutes at a time. There was one corner of the kitchen where he apparently lurked. There Mouser would prance, box, jump and pounce exactly as if she were playing with another cat. They had even wilder games in the dining room. We have seen Mouser follow something round with her eyes as it apparently ran behind the pieces of furniture. Then she would stalk the Little Man cautiously, wait until he emerged, and pounce on him.

Mouser walked out of the house one winter's night and has never been seen since. Perhaps the Little Man lured her away.

The relationship between the cats and the peafowl is an interesting study. Ignorant and forward kittens have been known to play with Lucifer's tail. He doesn't care for this, and will jerk it away, but he is gentle and will never harm the kittens. Sometimes he will even try to teach them to pick up food from the ground. And if no other birds are around he will bend down, fix the kitten with a beady eye, and invite conversation.

But the peahens are another matter. All our cats have learnt — through bitter experience when young — that to advance on a peahen, even tentatively and out of friendly curiosity, is to invite an attack. The hen will fan out her tail and jump heavily on the cat — and they are no lightweights. Now the cats give the hens a wide berth. It is amusing to watch one of the cats skirting round a group of peafowl. Dignity forbids her to break into a run, much as she would like to, but she casts apprehensive glances over her shoulder. Once she is out of the danger zone she obviously feels she has been made to look foolish, and embarrassment causes her to sit down and give herself a rapid wash.

In relation to the peafowl the mallard, for all their intelligence, have never learned caution. They rush forward with noisy enthusiasm to join the peafowl at meals, and several of their number invariably get heavily jumped upon. Luckily it doesn't seem to hurt them in the least; but it makes meal times rather restless. As any observer of bird life will have noticed, among the more belligerent birds it is considered more important to stop your inferiors from getting food than to eat it yourself.

34 ❧ ALTHOUGH by now we feel competent to rear the peachicks to maturity — barring accidents — and to deal with any incidence of disease, during most breeding seasons there is usually some crisis which threatens the safety either of the eggs or of the chicks.

On two occasions last year something frightened the birds when the chicks were still very young and roosting in the old apple tree in the orchard. We were away the first time it happened, and four chicks disappeared. Although the whole Selby family searched every foot of our property, they never found any trace of a peachick. They had probably flown right off our land, and were too small to survive alone. This tragedy left Matilda and Priscilla with only six chicks between them.

The second alarm occured when we had been home for a week. We were wakened at five o'clock in the morning by the frantic honking of the peahens. We fell out of bed, pulled on a few clothes and, still half asleep, we staggered out into the garden. We found Priscilla wandering round the orchard, croaking her heart out, while Matilda was perched at the top of a tall elm tree, also in a state of lamentation. There wasn't a chick to be seen anywhere.

Still feeling dazed, we started in the half light what seemed a hopeless search for the six chicks, who were still very small.

Matilda is a sensible bird, and she soon flew down out of the elm tree and started calling to the chicks. While we were pacing the garden from end to end, two chicks flew down out of two different trees and joined their mother. Then John heard a faint croak and found a third chick crouching under a hedge in the kitchen garden, which he caught quite easily. I found one in a ditch in the farmer's field. I only managed to catch this one because it soon became too exhausted to fly.

Our farmer neighbour, who was now up and about, re-ported seeing 'an odd looking little owd bird' on top of one of his barns. This was some way from our garden, and we felt doubtful if we should ever round this one up, if it *was* a pea-chick.

Feeling more exhausted than the chicks, we tottered over to the big barn, where we found number five perched on top, croaking hoarsely. This capture promised to be more difficult than the others, and we had to make a plan of campaign. John threw small clods of earth at it to drive it down, while I tried to see in which direction it flew. If it had flown towards the road we should have lost it, but it flew right across the big stackyard and luckily landed in a bed of nettles close to our fence. Between us we were able to catch it. Our hands were badly stung, but that seemed a cheap price to pay for the chick. We had had neither sight nor sound of the sixth chick, and at six o'clock we decided to go back to bed and try to get an hour's sleep.

Still fast asleep at seven o'clock, we didn't see Mrs. Selby coming down the drive, carrying something with great care. But she was bursting with news when we saw her later in the morning. She told us that her brother-in-law had come in to say that there was a young pheasant in their stackyard. Mrs. Selby took one look and laughed scornfully. 'That be'ant no pheasant. That'ull be a peacock from the Manor,' she said. 'Now you men all get out of the way, dew you'll frit it.'

Having disposed of her men-folk, Mrs. Selby ran into the house, quickly hard-boiled her breakfast egg, chopped it up and scattered it by the peachick. As it was eating hungrily, she pounced on it, picked it up, carried it round here and put it down with its brothers and sisters. We were full of admiration for her initiative and quick thinking. It was certainly our lucky morning. What had sparked off the crisis in the first instance we never discovered.

There was an alarming and dramatic incident this last summer which might have lost Matilda all her eggs. She had been sitting on six eggs for about a week, comfortably ensconced under a hedge in the big paddock — a more sensible nesting place than some she has previously chosen. One morning we heard Priscilla hooting in alarm — she had not yet started sitting. Knowing how the hens become hysterical on the least provocation, we didn't hurry out to see what the trouble was until we heard Lucifer screaming.

When we reached the paddock we saw Priscilla running round and round Matilda's nest in a state of great agitation. Lucifer, equally agitated, and shrieking loudly, was also running round, but at a safe distance from the trouble spot. When we were close enough we saw Matilda standing straddled over her eggs.

She, alone of the birds, wasn't making a sound. She was delivering hammer blows with her beak at some large black object that was moving just outside her nest. As we rushed to the nest the black thing gave a violent jerk and then lay still. But Matilda was leaving nothing to chance. With relentless fury she was still hammering at what we now saw was an enormous carrion crow.

It was stone dead, pecked right through the eye, but Matilda didn't think so, and we had some difficulty in getting the crow away from her. I have never seen a bigger carrion crow, and if I hadn't seen the result of the battle with my own eyes I would have backed the crow to win every time.

It is obvious that Matilda was just about to leave the nest for her daily rest-period when the crow attacked. Perhaps it had been watching from a nearby tree, with its eye on the eggs. It flew down a little too soon for its health. None of the eggs was damaged in the fight, and luckily the attack didn't put Matilda off sitting — if anything, she seemed more perky than usual. No doubt she was 'whully proud' of her victory.

35 ❧ I SUPPOSE it is a sign of increasing age, but it seems to me that Christmas comes more quickly every year. We are suddenly told — in every newspaper and on every hoarding — that there are only so many 'clear shopping days' left. Usually I haven't done any shopping at all, and I become panic-stricken. Apart from the shopping, there are the Christmas cards to send off. We are usually so late with this task that those destined for foreign countries have to be sent by Air Mail — very expensively and uneconomically — and, I suppose — typical of us.

However, once we have sent off our cards and posted our parcels, and when I have broken the back of the shopping and, by immense efforts of organization unnatural to me, have managed to subdue my panic, we enjoy every minute of Christmas and the preparations for it. Our attitude to Christmas, I should say at once, is wholly traditional and wholly 'square'.

It always seems to me that one of the basic Christmas chores is the setting out of the many Christmas cards we seem to receive. These start arriving during the second week in December. Their disposal is no problem at first, because we stand them on top of bookshelves and on window sills. They look particularly appropriate against the leaded window panes. Invariably, however, they blow down immediately anyone opens a door.

Once the obvious places are filled up, John has to be encouraged to get up on a chair and fix — with the aid of drawing pins — lines of ribbon along the ceiling beams in all the rooms. From then on it is my job to fill up these lines by sticking a piece of cellotape to the card and attaching it to the ribbon. One of the most tiresome hazards of this operation is the way the free end of the cellotape seems to get lost. It becomes firmly and invisibly re-stuck onto its roll. Even if I can find the join and prise it up with a finger nail, it is impossible to tell which way it wants to unroll. By now I am gibbering, and rush to John. He has a way with cellotape.

Last Christmas was a particularly gay and happy one. Jeremy and Maureen and our two grandsons, Heywood and Patrick, were due to arrive on Christmas Eve, so we had set up and decorated the Christmas Tree the day before. We have the Tree in the Garden Room, as there is plenty of space there for the children to play without knocking a decoration off the Tree every few minutes. All our presents are put in individual heaps on a bed of pine branches round the Tree.

When the family arrived about six o'clock nearly everything was organized. I say 'nearly everything' advisedly, as I remember I had a pile of gifts in my closet waiting to be wrapped and labelled later in the evening. But a meal was prepared, and wood fires were roaring in the big open hearths, and reflections of the flames were dancing on the red berries of the holly and the dark green leaves of the ivy with which we had decorated the rooms. The whole scene, in fact, was almost unbelievably in accordance with the conventions of the Victorian Christmas card.

The two little boys were, of course, in a state of great excitement. Not only was there the ritual hanging-up of the Christmas Stocking for them to look forward to, but they were to stay up to an early dinner. After dinner we were expecting one of the most significant events of our Christmas — the arrival of the village choir to play carols on handbells.

Somewhere there may exist better handbell ringers than ours — although I have yet to hear them — but there can be no ringers alive who put more enthusiasm into their ringing or produce a more joyous sound. The choir consists of about twelve people, of both sexes and of all ages, from youngsters of about nine years old to married couples.

On arrival they ring one carol outside our front door, gathered round a large lantern. It is a rigid convention that we all stay seated — and silent — inside the house until the first carol is ended. But it is much easier for them to see the music clearly if they come inside the house, and it is much more fun for us if we can see them ringing. So after this first carol they all come inside and troop through into the Garden Room.

Last Christmas Eve we were a particularly receptive audience. The Grampions had come round to listen to the carols with us, and so had our great friends and nearest neighbours, Hugh and Juliet Edwards. They have now, alas, moved out of Suffolk, and the knowledge that this was the last Christmas they would be with us lent poignancy to the evening. We managed to find chairs for the grown-ups. The two boys, ready for bed and clad in pyjamas and dressing-gowns, squatted on the floor.

Heywood and Patrick had not heard the bell-ringers before. They sat absolutely still, for once, lost in wonder, while the choir played us all the old favourites from *In Dulce Jubilo* to 'While Shepherds Watched'. I was torn between the pleasure of watching my grandsons and enjoying the look of fierce concentration and determination on the faces of some of the younger ringers.

The choir seemed to enjoy ringing the handbells as much as we enjoyed listening. But when they had finished 'Come All Ye Faithful' I thought the youngest ringer looked a little tired, so I suggested a break for refreshments.

We had prepared for this break as far as possible beforehand. We had orangeade for the youngest, and then we advanced through Pepsi-Cola to beer, sherry or whisky for the older members. Everyone sat on the floor. While we passed round the drinks, Heywood and Patrick offered Christmas cake and mince pies, putting the plates on the floor while they examined the handbells, giving them a good shake with considerably less success than their owners. Some of the younger members of the choir are always shy at first, but this does not last long, and they are soon chatting away as fast as mouthfuls of plum cake will let them.

When all have eaten and drunk their fill the choir staggers to its feet. During this operation some of the younger ones invariably knock their glasses over and their faces turn a bright scarlet. We pretend not to notice.

John then hands over our gift of money — it usually goes for repairs to the church roof — to the oldest member of the choir, and he makes a short speech thanking them for the entertainment. At this point they always insist on ringing one more carol for us. How some of the children can manage this energetic exercise after all they have eaten and drunk amazes me.

As a *finale* the choir played for us 'Hark The Herald Angels Sing' and then they filed out, amidst a chorus of conventional sentiments, giggles, and remarks upon the excellence of the cake. Our two little grandsons, by now thoroughly overexcited, were with difficulty prevented from following them down the drive. However, we reminded them that they had to hang up their stockings, so they went upstairs with their mother, and we promised to go up and say 'good-night' to them later.

We were left to have a quiet drink with our friends. So powerful is the Spirit of Christmas — gently aided, of course, by another sort of spirit — that we were able to sit and contemplate with equanimity a floor littered with crumbs, a pool of orangeade, and the shattered fragments of two of my best wine glasses.

36

WE ALWAYS spend Christmas Day quietly, and I don't suppose our day is very different from that of millions of other people. We always feel, however, that there is something rather special about Boxing Day when, shortly before noon, we have a gathering of those families whose life is very much bound up with the house in which we live.

By noon on Boxing Day we women hope we have cooked our last hot meal for the time being. As we propose to feed our families on nothing but cold turkey for the next few days, Mrs. Selby, her daughter Dulcie and I myself all feel free to relax and enjoy ourselves without feeling we have to hurry back to the kitchen.

This Christmas we were a larger party than usual. Mrs. Selby's widowed brother, Edwin, had recently come to live with her, so of course we had asked him to join the party. Mrs. Selby, Henry and Edwin were the first arrivals. Henry Selby looked spruce but unfamiliar, wearing a collar and tie — we seldom see him in other, than his working clothes. Dulcie arrived next, with her husband and their five children. By the time we had them all seated round the Christmas Tree, the younger children on the floor, Alfred had joined us, looking smart in a dark blue suit, his hair plastered down, and giving us his usual rather hesitant grin.

This party, like our carol party, does need some organizing, but it is easier in every way. The children all like Pepsi-Cola, and our grown-up visitors — who usually drink beer — on this occasion all drink sherry.

Now that there are so many of us present the ice is broken more quickly, conversation is soon flowing easily, and no one has to make any effort. Our presents to the Selbys, to Dulcie and her family, and to Alfred, are still waiting under the Tree, and so are their presents to us. So we start an orgy of unwrapping parcels, eating mince pies and pulling crackers. In between times Heywood puts the record of a carol on the record player and we all make a noise that we hope is singing.

A party that started twelve years ago with two children now has seven — although Mrs. Selby's two elder grandsons have left school and would not like to be called children any more. I had no very original thoughts as I looked round at their excited, well-scrubbed faces, while they opened their parcels. I just felt amazement at the rapidity with which time passes. I also felt an intense gratitude that John and I had weathered two World Wars and more than thirty-three years of marriage, and were here together, looking on this familiar and unvarying scene.

To me, one of the charms of Christmas is that every year it *should* repeat a familiar pattern — that, broadly speaking, every scene should be recognizable. It gives a sense of continuity in a fast-changing world, and I think children particularly enjoy and appreciate this, even if unconsciously.

Jeremy has long since exhausted his supply of practical jokes, but this Christmas the seven-year-old Heywood produced a fake chocolate, which Alfred, although he recognized it from of old, accepted and attempted to bite, with the required expression of consternation.

As the sherry was passed round for the second time, and tongues were loosened, I listened to much the same jokes and badinage, to the same recollections of life on the farm, that I had listened to every Boxing Day for the past twelve years.

Once again, also, I observed Mrs. Selby's rising impulse to get to her feet and deliver her annual speech. I knew from past experience that by the time she was halfway through her second glass of sherry she found the call to get up and speak almost irresistible. Today her restraint was something of a record. So I made a diversion by proposing the toast of Mrs. Selby, 'without whom we couldn't live here.' That is a true statement.

Puss-in-Boots gets the Christmas Spirit

White Christmas

A little red in the face, but steady as a rock, Mrs. Selby heaved herself to her feet. Holding her glass aloft she in turn proposed our health. Her speech is, thank goodness, always the same. Although I blush to write it, she says that John and I are the best neighbours in the world.

'We all know,' she says, 'that Mr. and Mrs. Hadfield would give us the chimney-pots off their housen if we needed them.' Then she thanks us for the party and for the presents, and she ends by expressing the hope that we will live at the Manor forever.

Dear, devoted, unique Mrs. Selby! I question whether the first part of her speech is wholly justified. But we *would* give her our chimney-pots if there were any on our chimneys. And I hope that her hope for the future is fulfilled for as long as 'forever' lasts for John and me.

37 ❧ ALTHOUGH Christmas is over there is a mellow, autumnal feeling about today that reminds me of that day, more than twelve years ago, when we first stood on the lawn, that was then neither spacious nor sweeping, and gazed — still a trifle incredulously — at our Manor house. The sun is surprisingly warm today, but there is a nip in the air. Great billowy white clouds drift slowly across the vast East Anglian sky, and are reflected in the calm water of the moat. There is no sound but the distant, contented grunting of the Selbys' pigs, who have just been fed, and, nearer at hand, the cheerful song of a robin in the Strawberry Tree that still regularly presents its rosy fruits at Christmas time.

These twelve years have passed with incredible swiftness. I feel as if I have barely had time to unpack and get straight. I suppose that in their ups-and-downs they much resemble twelve years in the lives of most ordinary folk. We have had our periods of worry and anxiety; some of our problems were objective, and many were the result of our being the particular fallible people we are. I think we have had rather more than our share of luck, despite what people say about peacock feathers, and we have certainly experienced times of great happiness and contentment.

We can stand on the lawn that is now spacious and sweeping — even if it does grow plantains particularly well — and see that most of the yew hedges we planted have grown shoulder high, and are looking massive but shapely. The box hedge still has some way to go, but is flourishing, and so is the Catalpa tree we planted near-by.

I fear that our grandchildren will be the only ones to see the holly hedge looking exactly as we planned it — it has suffered some vicissitudes. But the weeping willow we planted by the moat two years ago has grown extraordinarily quickly. Its slender, drooping branches sway gracefully in the wind — a lovely shimmering golden-green against the darker green of the yew hedge beyond. The Irish yews we put in the walled garden stand proudly erect, over eight feet high, and ivy and clematis have now climbed to the top of the brick wall.

Our kitchen garden stands apart, surrounded by a dense Myrobalan plum hedge which is supposed (erroneously) to prevent the peafowl from sharing our taste in tender lettuce and green peas. Like our predecessors we harvest vast quantities of Blenheim Orange Pippins from an ancient tree beside the moat, and there is now a substantial yield from apple trees which were only two or three feet high when we planted them — Orleans Reinette, Egremont Russet, and D'Arcy Spice.

We can look at the old house with some pride and satisfaction, knowing that it is at least sound, with repointed brickwork and all the beautiful octagonal chimneys repaired. Nearly all the windows now have leaded lights, and the refashioning of the ugly Victorian annexe into a garden room, overlooking and partly enclosing the little courtyard, has made the back of the house a peculiarly satisfying architectural group.

The wistaria has nearly covered the back wall and has grown up to the roof; the espalier pear tree growing against the South gable has now passed the first floor windows, and the vine we planted against the West gable-end — where tradition has it that there has always been a vine — climbs steadily up the house and now bears grapes.

There are still a few things to be done. There is a blocked window to be opened up. Another window has to be reconstructed, with the correct number of lights. Whether or not the day will come when we have to spend £500 on the roof, as gloomily forecast by our original Builder, remains to be seen.

We haven't, at this very moment, got an overdraft at the Bank. On the strength of this John has drawn up elaborate plans for remodelling a large part of the inside of the house, so

131

that we can replace our relatively modern staircase with a massive one of ancient oak which he picked up in a builder's yard some years ago and has been hoarding ever since. He showed me these plans last night with pride.

They are excellent plans, but the temporary absence of an overdraft does not necessarily mean a permanent surplus of cash. I tried to point this out to John, and said I would settle for a simple and modest remodelling of my kitchen.

38

I HAVE just been to answer the back door bell, thinking it was the butcher. To my surprise there was a lorry standing in the drive. The man at the door handed me an invoice. 'One thousand secondhand red bricks,' he said, 'Where do you want them?'

I took the invoice to John in the library. 'What *is* this all about?' I asked.

He had the grace to look a little sheepish. 'Oh, well,' he said, 'they seemed so very cheap, and bricks are jolly scarce now. After all, we did promise ourselves a gazebo. I've worked out exactly how it would fit in the corner of the wall round the moat garden.'

'Go and look after your wretched bricks then,' I said crossly. '*I* have promised myself a two-thousand-pound swimming pool in the corner of the paddock.'

It seems that we are still very much the same people we were twelve years ago. Perhaps, as a result, our existence in this lovely old place is as precarious as it was then. Never mind; we *are* still here; we are happy; and today there are nine peacocks on the lawn.